# Up Home Again

## A Memoir

## Ellie O'Leary

North Country Press

Up Home Again

Copyright © 2023 by Ellie O'Leary

Cover photo by Mary Morrison

ISBN 978-1-943424-79-5

North Country Press
Unity, Maine

To my friends and family – especially Alwina, Carol, Cathy, and Martha who helped me get through these times and to Gavin and Ananda who might never have heard any of this if I hadn't written it down.

# Contents

# Prologue

## The Upheavals

"Honey, Mommy's gone. God wanted her."
With those words from my sister Jo, everything was changed.
What I knew was no more. Not as I had known it.
"He wanted her?" I thought. "With all the dead people he already has, he gets my mother? I'm not done with her yet."
On February 7, 1959, she was gone. She was fifty-six. I was ten.
I became The Little Girl Who Didn't Need a Mother Anyway.

I would be the girl who could sew my own clothes, bake my own bread, and tie my own shoes. I would do for myself what my mother had done. I could actually tie my own shoes but, the other things that I couldn't do for myself, I decided I didn't really need to do.

We'd been living in Freedom, Maine, for only a few months when my mother died. My two older sisters stayed in Massachusetts, but I lived in Freedom Village with my father and older brother, Danny.

Some girls were like a little princess, others more like a tomboy. I was kind of a . . . well, I don't know if there was a name for it. I was a lonely girl.

I grew up wanting to travel, to get an education, and a family. At different times I fancied myself becoming a lead singer in a rock group, a powerhouse of a businesswoman, or a war correspondent. I didn't want a war, so I changed that last one to travel journalist.

I looked at things - a rock, a car, a tree - and wondered why they were still around and my mother was gone. My father let me get a cat; I would look at it and wonder why it was alive. I didn't like losing things, didn't take disappointments well, and cried when criticized. I tried to train myself to think normal things, to see things as they really were, not as I feared.

I saw that other people's parents could go into the hospital and come home alive. It could happen if my father got sick. The first semester of my freshman year in college, my father was admitted to Togus Veteran's Hospital in Augusta, Maine. He died. He was sixty-three. I was eighteen. That ended our already less than good relationship.

Despite doing everything my own way without much of an outline, I did manage to graduate from college, travel, get married, and was raising a family when what I knew and how I knew it changed again.

Breast cancer came, then bankruptcy, then divorce, then breast cancer again. What I had left was gratitude for three healthy children who loved me and each other, for friends to help me, and for my own freelance style that was going to have to get me through this next episode of starting over.

## 2004

*A sharp, indrawn breath,*
*half groan, half acceptance,*
*that means "Life's like that.*
*We know it (also death)."*

"The Moose"
Elizabeth Bishop

No need to go crazy looking for things as I pack and unpack. I may already have crossed that line anyway. Even though this move back to Maine is difficult for me, I plan to keep it organized.

The first thing I move into my son Matthew's house is my fabric collection. Trying to maintain some sense of control, I need to make sure my fabrics, at least, are secured. I have sorted them into large plastic bins according to my own sense of order, based on a combination of fiber content, weight, knit vs. woven, and color. Matt has been working nights so I wake him up the afternoon I arrive at his house in Kittery, Maine, my dark green Ford Escape loaded with this personal cargo. He has grown up with fabric; he once went to a middle school Halloween dance dressed as a basketball. He knows who sewed the brown vinyl then stretched it over a frame made by his dad.

His only question today is, "Where do you want them, Mom?" as he unloads.

"Could they please go in the house, not the garage?" I don't want my silks to be out alone all night.

No longer my little basketball boy, Matt with his six-foot frame, carries the bins easily. Now in his late twenties, with a degree in mechanical engineering, he works on nuclear submarines; but still makes time for his mother. Our relationship is strong; he has been a support for me through my troubles of the last few years.

The woolens, the novelties, the cottons, the whole collection, stacked neatly, takes up a good portion of a first-floor room no one is using. We also set up my computer in there, making me feel grounded somewhere, at least for the month or so I will be staying here. I will be moving back up to Maine's Waldo County, moving in with my friend Martha, but not yet.

Since Matt's house is only half an hour away from where I have been living in Massachusetts, my transition begins here. He had been renting this big house with a few other guys in their twenties, but now in May 2004 there's only one housemate left, and that young man is away for a few months.

Although I'm moving, I haven't given up my two jobs yet. I am still showing real estate as well as working part time at a group home for mentally and physically challenged women. Moving is piecemeal and I'm not sure what I want to keep and what I want to throw away. My other two children, Luke and Brigid, are getting a good portion of my furniture and the rest is going into Matt's garage or the trailer meant for hauling his racing motorcycle.

Since 1996 I have gone through divorce, bankruptcy, and two bouts of breast cancer. Now eight years out from the onset of all that, I finally give in. My finances have crashed. Managing a full-time real estate career has become an experience of feast or famine and the famines are getting closer together. I haven't been able to keep up with my car payments, my rent, or my credit cards. I've lost. I've lost my home, my health, my pride. I've lost the battle. I might have to surrender, at least for a while.

Getting paid strictly on commission with lots of business expenses in between sales, has left me broke. I tried to keep working but, needing immediate income not potential, the real estate thing is way too much for me. Initially I tell my clients I'm taking a leave of absence after the morning one man left me a message around 7 a.m.

"Ellie, I want to see that land in Brentwood. I'll meet you there at ten this morning."

At ten, he leaves me another message. "Ellie, I'm here. Where are you?"

Through the wonders of electronics, I get both messages at 10:15. This is the sort of thing that happens and at one time wouldn't have upset me so much, but now I know I can't handle it anymore. Not many days later, I make the leave of absence permanent knowing I may again work in and around real estate or write about it, but vowing I will never again be a real estate agent.

Every day Matt comes home from work in the morning. Checking the mail doesn't occur to me because the mailbox is across the street, a busy road. Anyway it's not my mail. Most of the drama in my life right now is my own until Matt opens his mail one morning saying, "Whoa, Mom, Nana Beulah died."

My first thought is she couldn't have died, my friend Suzanne would have told me, but he is standing in his kitchen reading a note from Suzanne. Her mother, the woman he has always known as Nana Beulah, has died. With the funeral over, Suzanne is sending out notes. Getting this news makes my insides wrench. Beulah dying is real life, but finding out this way makes me feel so detached to learn I hadn't even known about it.

Matt and I talk, going over some memories of Beulah and her husband Channing.

To my kids, they were Nana Beulah and Grandpa Channing because Suzanne's parents took a liking to me or just felt sorry for me when they met me at Bates College in Lewiston, Maine, when Suzanne and I were freshmen. Each time her parents came up from Cape Cod to visit her, they'd take her out to breakfast on Sunday morning. When they realized there were no parents to do the same for me, I started getting invited to those Sunday breakfasts, too. I loved it. The relationship grew until eventually I used to visit them at their home whether or not Suzanne was there.

They were real people from Wellfleet, not the summer crowd from New York. When Wellfleet became The Art Capital of the Outer Cape, they were still real people. Once in the '70s when a bunch of us were visiting, the weekend included an invitation to an opening at one of the local galleries. It probably wasn't called New York Meets Real People, but that was my interpretation of the theme. Suzanne had been a long-time babysitter for some of the New York people and one of them had done a film with accompanying photos of the local population. We all trooped in, about seven of us. There were large artworks on the walls of the small gallery. Suzanne and I both knew we added some of the local color in person. Although we were a little silly going into the place, we were trying to behave ourselves.

Beulah, on the other hand, must have been a bit intimidated. A tall woman with a shock of white hair, she was not naive or uneducated. She had been a second-grade teacher for years, but she could be shy among adults. She was the one who tripped up, and I mean literally. Jostling for space just when I thought we had all angled our way in uneventfully, Beulah managed to knock one of the large paintings off the wall. Once Suzanne and I made eye contact our best behavior was over. The scene became Country Cousins Go to the Art Gallery. Her father Channing, an infinitely helpful mechanic with a crew cut and a smile, tried to help rehang the painting. The New York people were gracious, almost solicitous, trying to say what happened was okay. Suzanne and I, fighting off laughs but bordering on embarrassment, headed for the wine and cheese while the film began to roll in the background in a continuous loop. By then, though, who needed a film? We had just shown up in person.

Now Beulah is dead, I live nowhere, and it hurts.

I'm scheduled to be at my job at the group home today from 3-11 p.m. so I go off to work. The women who live there make great companions. Working in their home, preparing dinner, assisting with personal needs and just being there for them is a good diversion. By 11 p.m. though I'm tired when I set out on the drive back to Matt's house. I listen to NPR, but at this hour they're playing something that sounds to me like bedtime music. I'm afraid I'll fall asleep so I push scan for something more lively, but not so raucous it hurts my ears.

The house is quiet and dark when I get back since Matthew is working the night shift, doing something on or near a submarine. I'm alone. I turn on lights as I cross the first floor heading for the space where my stuff is, to check my email one last time before bed. I think of making a cup of tea; I'm okay until I get to the center of the room. I'm headed for my computer but when I look left along the far wall, I see my whole fabric collection is gone. Gone. Empty floor space. Blank wall.

There's no one to ask. It's almost midnight. My first thought is someone came home and threw my fabrics away thinking they were just boxes of rags. This used to be some housemate's room. Maybe he came back to clean up. Maybe he thought this stuff could be in the house, but not this room.

Trying to be organized about this, I start at the top. I check the attic where the boys have set up a game room, but there are no fabrics up there. Mustering up the courage to check the basement even though the light is out, I go down with a big blue flashlight. I've never been down here before since it's an old house where I have no interest in the basement. Shining the flashlight around me, I use it to break cobwebs as I progress. Why would anyone put anything down here? There's lots of old junk, but it looks like it's been here for years. No fabrics. Scrambling out of the basement as if a monster might be chasing me up the stairs, I'm still desperate for my fabric collection.

After checking all the rooms in the house, I decide to look outdoors. First I head for Matt's motorcycle trailer where part of my household is stored. Still with big blue flashlight in hand, I undo the padlock and try to release the back door without getting hurt. It comes down at me to form a ramp, but I'm afraid if I let it go, I'll break it. If I try to let it down gently, it might break me. The door is heavy for me to handle anyway but tonight my anxiety makes the task almost too big. Once I do manage to get the door open, I see some of the same stuff I expect to see just inside the trailer. I don't see my plastic bins of fabric.

My next hope is the garage. To open it, I have to go back inside the house to use the automatic door opener sitting on the kitchen windowsill. I think the thing only works sometimes because it only works sometimes for me. Matt has explained I don't point it correctly. Tonight I point well; one side of the garage opens up right away. It's dark out so I cross the driveway with the flashlight, flicking on the light inside when I get there. The garage has bicycles, tools, motorcycles, camping gear, and lots of guys' toys and rubbish that looks like junk to me. It all belongs to Matt, his current housemate, previous residents, and who knows who else. Guys have moved in, moved out, and left stuff. Along one side of the garage there are some bureaus, small tables, and luggage belonging to me. There is still no sign of my fabrics.

By now my anxiety has twisted into hysteria heading toward despair. I'm crying out loud. I want my fabrics: I've given up enough. My mother was the first one to teach me anything about sewing, but she died when I was ten. When I was becoming a mother for the first time, I took it up again and have become good at it on my own. I don't want to lose my fabrics, not tonight.

Thinking for a moment a cup of tea will help everything, then thinking a cup of tea will help nothing, I decide to check the attic and the basement another time, as much as I don't want to. I check the motorcycle trailer again and redo my search in the garage. Still no fabrics. There is one more place. Next to the garage is an open shed where the boys have hung plastic trash bags, overhead, so animals won't get to the rubbish and garbage inside. Animals, probably raccoons, have attacked these bags. Now it's approaching 1 a.m. on a dark, dark night. I'm shining my big blue flashlight ahead of me so I don't walk into any of these black, plastic, dripping smelly remains. No fabrics. I don't want them to be in here, but I want my fabrics.

When I go back inside the house, I wash up and make myself that cup of tea, before I do the rounds once more. This time when I search the trailer, I bother to shine the flashlight deep inside, checking not just the end where new things would be put, but the whole space. There at the opposite end I see the corner of a cloudy, translucent plastic bin with its white lid. They're there. They're all there. Plaids, linens, sheers, and even my daughter Brigid's skating fabrics. I have them.

Matt has repacked the trailer in a more efficient manner for when he will make the trek further north to Martha's house in Monroe. Where I might have just put the fabrics inside the trailer, he unpacked and rearranged the whole thing. A few days later after he told his girlfriend, Gretyl, the story, she asks him "Why did your mother get so upset?"

He explains in his succinct manner, "She couldn't find her fabrics, and besides, someone's mother died."

# Upheaval

This move back to Maine is the continuation of the turmoil that began in the summer of 1996 when the second major upheaval of my life began. I coughed one day. As my right hand brushed against my chest, I happened to notice a lump in my left breast and I knew enough to make a doctor's appointment. He examined me, said it was probably a cyst, and told me to come back in a month to see if there were any changes. I went away for a week that month, to my first writing retreat, with what felt like a small stone in my breast.

For my next appointment, the office was busy. Too busy. I wanted to get in and out of there on my way to work at a mortgage company, but the morning wasn't going as I had planned. When I told the receptionist I had been waiting way past my appointment time, she said the doctor was working alone and a few women had gone into labor. I wanted to mention I had a lump in my breast, but I felt that was too much melodrama. I asked if I could reschedule.

She said, "Yes, take a seat and we will call you."

"To reschedule?"

"Yes, I don't do the scheduling."

I told her, "No, thank you," and left.

I went to work, but I still had a lump and still needed to do something. I called Beth Israel Hospital in Boston and asked for a referral to a gynecologist who no longer did obstetrics, since I no longer needed that specialty.

For my first appointment with my new doctor, I was looking for someone to tell me not to worry, everything would be fine. He said it looked like a cyst and he would aspirate it right then and there.

"Little pinch."

Why do they always say that?

# Upheaval

"We'll see if we can drain it and send you on your way."

Perfect, I thought. Make the thing disappear.

He inserted the needle and pulled out a syringe full of nice, red blood. Even I knew cysts do not have a blood supply. This thing growing in me had a life of its own. Before I left his office, I was scheduled for surgery two days later to remove the deviant growth.

My husband, with his father, was in California visiting his brother, so my friend Carol dropped me off at the hospital. I figured: cut it out, examine it, and we'll go from there. I was sort of awake during the surgery under anesthesia called MAC. I heard the doctor say it was bigger than he expected, but he thought he got it all.

I did wonder what difference it would make to get it all, if it's a cyst. I hadn't even left the operating room, but I was realizing, it wasn't as simple as a cyst. I was forty-eight years old. If I could make it to fifty-six, everything after that would be gravy. From the age of fifty-six on, I'd be living the years my mother never had.

Another friend, Cathy, picked me up after the surgery and the ride home would have been pretty uneventful, if I hadn't thrown up on her. I felt it coming, told her so, and she pulled over. She also reached across me to open the door and that's when I lost it. She was driving my car; so at least I only got her, not her vehicle. At home I rested and felt okay, not energetic. I still didn't have the official result of the biopsy; that would come a few days later.

The evening after the surgery my husband and his father returned. When my father-in-law saw me stretched out on the living room sofa, he asked if I felt okay. I said I was getting better.

"From what?" he asked.

"From surgery. I had a lump removed yesterday."

We both shot a look at my husband. I had spoken to him on the phone at his brother's house. He knew all this was happening.

"You didn't say anything," his father scolded him.

"I didn't want to answer a lot of questions." He had continued his vacation without a word on the unfolding situation back home.

# Upheaval

A few days later in the post-surgical visit, my doctor let me know how things were going to be now. "You're healing well, but unfortunately you'll need more treatment."

It was a gentle admission of a horrible truth. Leaving his office, I walked down eight flights of stairs because I was too agitated to wait for the elevator. From there I walked up Beacon Street in Brookline to my initial visit with my new surgeon. I don't remember anything this next doctor told me that day, but he seemed like a nice man – a sort of elder statesman of breast cancer. Before heading home, I went into Barnes and Noble to buy the fattest book I could find on my new situation, a topic that had been *other* as in other people's problem. Once it became my problem, I wanted to be able to step out of the vagueness and worry more specifically. Here at the onset of this upheaval, I read - as if to memorize - Dr. Susan Love's *Breast Book*, all one thousand plus pages. Sometimes I feel I've been tired ever since.

We had been married for twenty-one years and had three children when this news increased the strain on a strained marriage. I thought of cancer as a force to be reckoned with; he thought I made too big a deal out of it. He once heard my surgeon tell me, "I don't think you'll die from this, but we have you for life," and would remind me the doctor said I'm not going to die from it. Apparently, death would have been the necessary threat level required to get my husband's full attention.

I asked myself, "What if I knew I only had five years left? What would I change and why don't I change it now?"

I didn't make any immediate moves; I had no energy. We were on our way to becoming empty nesters with both sons away at college and our daughter in high school. Empty seemed to be the operative word.

The cancer diagnosis and treatment reignited a long-standing relationship I had with depression. I walked about in a cloud filled with emotion and fatigue. By the time I sought professional help, I could barely see through the mist. I might not have sought the level of treatment I received for the depression if it hadn't been for the cancer; but I might not have needed it right then either.

I was scheduled for seven rounds of chemotherapy to be administered intravenously in three-week intervals at Beth Israel Hospital. I was also going to be receiving six to seven weeks of radiation treatment. After I had the first three rounds of chemotherapy, I began the radiation, to be followed by the remaining chemo.

On the last day of my radiation treatments, a Tuesday, I went to the weekly breast cancer support group. By the time I got home about 7:30 p.m., Brigid was at a high school basketball game. She left a note congratulating me on finishing that phase of the treatment. My husband, as I expected, was already in bed asleep. After all, he needed to leave early for work every weekday morning.

A few days later I mentioned I had finished my radiation treatments on Tuesday. He said he knew.

"You didn't say anything, though. Brigie was out, but she left me a note."

"I was going to get you a cake."

"A cake?"

"Yeah, I stopped at the bakery in the grocery store to get a cake. I wanted them to put the international red circle of "NO" superimposed over the symbol for radiation."

"But you didn't?"

"No, they couldn't figure it out."

"But you didn't say anything."

"I tried to get you a cake, but they couldn't figure it out," he spoke more slowly and louder, as if to get the point across to someone more simple than himself.

"I didn't want a cake. I wanted you to say something."

"I tried, but they couldn't figure it out."

At this point he seemed totally frustrated with both them and me.

I said, "I have an idea. Why don't we split?"

"Why don't we."

We would have to sell our family home because of all the expenses connected with disease, kids in college, and divorce. He moved out sometime that summer. During Christmas break 1997

Upheaval

the kids and I moved from the four-bedroom turn-of-the-century home where they grew up into a two-bedroom place out near Lake Attitash in Amesbury. We went from a house where we always put the Christmas tree in the foyer to a cute, but small, place with a view. I got one bedroom; Brigid was still in high school, so she got the other. Luke, home from Simon's Rock College in Great Barrington, Massachusetts, had a dead-end hallway for his space and Matt slept on the fold-out couch. He was home from Syracuse University for the holidays even though he was spending his junior year in London.

The kids and I managed, with difficulty, in those first years of our new life. I worked a few different jobs as my health and stamina allowed --- managing a group home, writing as the town reporter for a local newspaper, and doing contract work for the mortgage company where I had worked a few years earlier. Eventually I would go back to full time real estate, the job I knew best.

Every year I went for the routine mammogram and in 1998, as I was being told everything's fine, I thought, "Good, but I wonder if some year that won't be true."

The next year I had my answer. In 1999 I was diagnosed a second time when a suspicious dot appeared on my mammogram. My friends Cathy and Carol swung into action. They set up the Ellie O'Leary Cancer Relief Fund, putting together a raffle where the tickets cost twenty-five dollars each even though I told them nobody would pay that much. I was wrong; they raised enough money to get me through the worst months in 1999 after the mastectomy. We all made it work, even my ex-husband increased child support. I scraped along believing I should be able to handle everything, and I mean everything, if I keep trying.

In the spring of 1997 my to-do list had consisted of cancer, house, divorce, and job. I tried to do all I was supposed to do concerning the cancer treatments including seeing a therapist; I listed our home for sale, started working out the details of the divorce, and wanted to leave my full-time job at the mortgage company. By the spring of 2004 I had been through everything on my list including my second bout with cancer. I had been laid off from my return to the mortgage company in between my second diagnosis and my surgery, so I had even changed jobs a few times. Good luck was not running with me, but I blamed myself for not being able to handle it all. Other people had bad luck, too. Other people had misfortunes. What was my problem? Why couldn't I handle everything all at once?

I did what I could, but I knew I was barely skimming the surface of doing okay. My to-do lists were scattered. Sometimes I worked on long-range plans - buy a house, travel abroad. Sometimes I worked on daily stuff - do the dishes, fold the laundry and, the perennial, clear up any clutter. My problem was I was not organized enough. I was sure of it. I was certain if I could get organized, I wouldn't be so tired.

*    *    *    *    *

I've been making the good effort for a few years, but now in the spring of 2004 I am worn down. The whole financial, medical, and personal process of my life has caught up with me. I am eroded. Due to what he terms my erratic payment history, my landlord is selling the little house I have been renting for six years. He apparently doesn't want to be a landlord anymore after dealing with the likes of me. I'm returning to Maine with credit card debt and a car loan that is too much for me. Fighting fatigue and depression is no way to run a real estate career. On the brink of personal implosion, I think about moving in with Martha, my high school friend who lives in the old farmhouse where she grew up. We met at Mount View, the regional high school. Although her home is in Monroe, about fifteen miles from Freedom where I lived, it is near enough to make me feel I am going up home again.

Making this decision has, for all of my adult life, been approximately Plan Z for me. Once I realize I have to move out of the lake house, I decide to really move. I can't imagine anyone in the town where I have been living would want me as a tenant. I am humiliated to the core.

Not knowing what else to do or where to go, I leave a message on Martha's answering machine to say I'll be moving in. This is hard. I shouldn't have to do this, but it is real. Martha is special; things don't bother her. It's no surprise when she calls back to tell me cheerfully that would be great as long as she doesn't have to cook and clean for me. I had almost forgotten to tell her my plans, so it is a relief to hear from her.

Eight years after my first cancer diagnosis and five years after the second, I am moving again. So far I have only made it as far as Matt's house in Kittery. I'm in the process of giving up my two jobs. I still have things back at the lake house and I've started to move things into Martha's, but her house is almost a three-hour drive from here. I wish I were settled in one place, that I lived somewhere for sure without any explanation to myself or anyone else. My books and most of my clothes are packed. Luke and Brigid, who are now sharing a house in western Massachusetts, are getting a good portion of my furniture and the rest is here at Matt's place. A lot of things I'm throwing away, as a sort of cleansing experience.

I'm not quite ready to leave Massachusetts and Martha isn't quite ready for me to move in. Her daughter, who has a two-year-old daughter of her own, recently returned from Georgia. Martha and I dropped her off there in January, because she was engaged to be married and, we thought, settled in the South. When she and her daughter came back to Maine in the spring, she announced the romance in Georgia was over. While Martha sorts that out, I am sorting through the mess, physical and emotional, that I am.

It's unsettling to be living with my son again, but this time in the home he shares with housemates. What seems embarrassing to me doesn't seem to faze him. Because he is working an overnight shift, I'm not in his way and the house is big enough. I do a few things mothers do in almost all circumstances. I do the dishes. I don't think he has done them this month.

# Beasts and Allergies

Some days I can't remember what I stored, what I kept near me. There is however the matter of my garden. I have not lost my garden. When I moved into the lake house in Amesbury, there were only a few perennials. Not wanting to mow any grass even on the tiny lot, I planted nearly everywhere except the driveway. This isn't merely a move; this is the end of my life in the town where I raised my family. My garden is alive, so I decide to take a good bit of it with me.

First I need a way to transport the plants in my car. Years ago in college I learned the term *functional fixedness* in psychology. With it a person could only imagine using something as it was originally intended. Going beyond such limitation, a person could envision a new use for a seemingly unrelated object. People do this all the time when they use a spoon handle or the blade of a dinner knife for a screwdriver. There are lots of examples that work, some that don't. Vases are not a good substitution for hammers. I've always felt a little surge of pride when I came up with a good way to overstep functional fixedness by demonstrating a down-to-earth creativity.

This is exactly how I feel the day I want to pack up my garden at the lake house and I spot the sleds. There are two plastic kids' sleds leaning up against the back of the house. The kids don't use them anymore, I have a lot of plants to dig up, and now I have two low, long plastic plant containers. Once I fill them with variegated hostas, day lilies, wild violets, and lots of variations of daisies and irises, among other things, I have most of my traveling garden packed.

The sleds are easy to slide into the back of my car especially since I still have the back seats down. My back seats haven't been upright for weeks since it is taking me most of April and even a little into May to move. At Matt's house I put the sleds behind the back steps keeping the flowers watered by running the hose right over the sleds themselves. There's no need to transplant, I won't be staying long. I add to my collection by "rescuing" some Johnny-jump-ups every time they pop up on Matt's lawn before the mowing people get there.

I also pack a lilac bush, a Mother's Day gift from Luke last year. We dig it up together replanting it into a blue plastic rubbish barrel too heavy for me to get in my car. Fortunately, my ex-husband is willing to go by the lake house to retrieve it. Once we get it all the way to Matt's house in Kittery, it joins the things that will one day make the trailer journey to Martha's house. Matt continues to pack the trailer efficiently, but I have to ask him to leave the lilac bush outside until the actual day of its trip north. He apparently understands physics better than gardening.

All of my stuff is thrown away, given away, stored at Matt's house or in my Ford Escape. I drive around for days with the remaining odds and ends from the lake house. I can see clothes hangers, baskets, and boxes whenever I get in and out of the car. I must look like a vagabond. I wish I were a carefree vagabond.

One fine weekend in early June I decide to drive my garden from Kittery to Monroe - except for the rubbish barrel potted lilac bush, which is too big for me to handle alone. I've sorted through all my things at Matt's house. I've thrown away some clothes, I have rediscovered some I hadn't worn for a long time, and I have thrown away nearly every piece of paper relating to my real estate career. With all that done, I am now driving my garden up home along the Maine Turnpike to its new soil.

This isn't the first trip of my move. I've already been to Martha's to organize my space in two back bedrooms. Martha's house is old and whatever little farmhouse it once was, it is now a rambling place rebuilt by committee. That committee would have been her father and his second wife, Alice, not Martha's mother. Neither of them is still living, so she has the place to herself with her daughter and granddaughter as sometime residents. Martha and I have much in common beyond high school. We were both born in Massachusetts and moved to Maine as children. We were both young when our mothers died and those mothers both came from Lowell, Massachusetts, although neither of us has ever lived there. Our mothers were not the same age and their families did not know each other.

Martha and her sister were in the same year in school; I was a year ahead of them. When three local high schools consolidated in the fall of 1964 into brand new Mount View High School, I met the two sisters, Martha and Alwina. I may say I grew up with them, but we were only together for my last two years of high school. Back in our day, you saw your friends in school but you pretty much did not see them over the summer unless they lived in the same town. Mount View drew its students from eleven towns covering about four hundred square miles. Martha and Alwina were not involved in any of our youthful escapades around Freedom Village or up at Freedom Pond.

After high school each of us migrated, eventually ending up in the Boston area. We were all married within about a year of each other and we each married a man at least a little bit younger than ourselves. We pretty much alternated in having our kids. Alwina went first with her daughter Kate and next I had Matthew. Among the three of us we ended up with seven kids altogether. When the kids were little, we visited back and forth, and they knew each other. Eventually with kids' activities, a few divorces, and moves we were still in touch but not close touch. One time when I was talking to Alwina she told me Martha had moved back to Monroe. That's brave, I thought. I was still haunted by my memories of the cold, not necessarily the weather, but the overwhelming sense of loss and grief I associated with any of Waldo County where the towns of Freedom and Monroe both lie. I told Alwina I couldn't do it. I couldn't move back to Maine.

Over the years, I had driven through the area a few times but only driven through, coming from something else like Thanksgiving with my brother when he lived in Orono, north of Waldo County. Actually, visiting and staying a few days would be something else, but that's what I was doing four years ago, on my first trip back after a long time, in April of 2000. I think of it now as my peace trip. I came back to visit Martha and to drive around some back roads. I started making a truce with the place that had haunted me, but never actually hurt me. On the Saturday of that first weekend visit, I decided to spend the whole day exploring the roads around Freedom. I hadn't planned this well; the last time I had done anything similar, it was on a bicycle. I quickly learned that in a car it doesn't take all day. Freedom is only eight miles from one end to the other, so on my big trip I also took in the nearby towns of Unity and Liberty. Honest. To get to Liberty from Freedom you have to go through Montville, but those are the real names of real places – all in Waldo County. Now I'm doing it. I'm moving back to Maine with components of my garden as passengers on this particular trip.

I've gardened a little bit at each of the places I've lived as an adult ever since, as a young married couple, we bought our first house, a triple-decker in the Dorchester neighborhood of Boston. There were plants there in the back of the yard that caused small welts to appear on my arms. It didn't bother me because they disappeared, usually in a matter of hours. After we moved to Amesbury, I gardened a little in that yard, too. Some plants there caused a red rash on my forearms. Again, it was a simple contact dermatitis that wore off quickly. I was able to keep gardening with no major effects, until I developed a disgusting sneezing and coughing problem.

In my real estate days, I was generally a well-dressed business-woman. Business casual would be an accurate description of my style, but I wasn't so casual that spitting up phlegm in public was anywhere near acceptable. In my forties I was diagnosed with allergies even though I didn't know that was possible. I thought you got allergies as a kid and kept them. When I went to a doctor who punched tiny holes in my back for testing with various substances, I found out I'm allergic to some things like mugwort, which I had never heard of before, as well as grass pollen and pine trees. Pine trees? I grew up in Maine! My path continued to advance from allergies to allergy-induced asthma with the occasional bronchitis until I got it under control.

Now I operate with a twice-daily pill along with three inhalers. Still it doesn't occur to me that packing my garden in the car and traveling for about three hours, with me and my plants, should be any problem. After all, I'm medicated; I have air conditioning.

During the trip I'm coughing and sneezing a bit, something I'm used to. By the time I hit Augusta, I'm coughing badly and take a detour, as usual, at a Dunkin Donuts drive-thru. I tell myself I need the coffee because I'm coughing so much. I like coffee. I like it a lot. From Augusta I head out on Route 3. It's not a divided highway; it's a long road going all the way to Belfast, the Waldo County seat, where it turns north heading along the coast. It's a good time for a cup of coffee. I'll be cutting off Route 3 early, way before Belfast, because I plan to take a left into Palermo at Tobey's Groceries, hang a left at a small obelisk, and then head straight into South Freedom. That will take me onto Route 137 thru Freedom Village up Knox Ridge and eventually into the town of Brooks by taking a left at exactly the right place. There are road signs up now, something new for us returnees. When we were kids you gave directions according to who lived in which house, but now almost forty years later, some of them have moved. From the town of Brooks, I'll take the Back Brooks Road into Monroe. All this may or may not be a shortcut from Augusta, but it is at least one more way to go.

Once I get to Martha's house, I know I'm in trouble. I'm coughing horribly and because I had a medium coffee, cream only, about an hour before the journey's end, I need to use the bathroom. It's good to be home, I think, and then remember, is this home? Is Kittery home? I'm finally where I am going tonight and there's a bathroom. Coughing, sneezing and nearly wetting myself, I get inside and ask Martha, "Why would anybody put their garden in a car and drive for a few hours?"

I take my flower sleds out of the back of my car to leave them outside in the cool night air. They're fine. I'm wheezing, but I have a rescue inhaler. I use it, take my other meds and turn in soon after Martha and I get caught up on the odds and ends of our lives. As long as I limit myself to breathing and sleeping, I figure I should be fine. One thing about this place, I sleep soundly even when I have trouble breathing.

The next day it's planting time. I can't leave the plants in the sleds. At Matt's house, I was around to water them, but I won't be staying here in Monroe. I have to go back to Kittery to get more of my things and I still work a few nights a week at the group home. These plants are not Martha's problem. Her idea of gardening is to let her father's tulips bloom then, once they've gone by, mow them down as part of the lawn. I brought these plants here and now I have to plant them. It's a misty day with patches of sunlight breaking out. It's a perfect day for gardening, not too hot or too dry, but I'm quickly reminded of one of Maine's tiniest beasts. The black flies are out.

Individual black flies are not obvious but they travel in large masses of nearly invisible little biting creature clans. They buzz so much even if they didn't bite, their presence would still be a kind of torture. It's not that they're loud; it's that they're there. Biting is, however, one of their greatest talents next maybe to squeezing into little nooks and crannies of your clothing where they don't belong. Today they are feasting. I'm sweaty, bothered, and occasionally sneezing loud enough to scare away black flies, along with other creatures, although the black flies keep coming back. I constantly hear a howl off in a pine stand near the house. It sounds like an injured cat. I pretty much know it's the trees bending as they do, but sometimes I think I might go see what it is. I decide if I do nothing, it is the trees. If I go over there it may be a bobcat, and then I'll wish I had done nothing. I keep planting even though the job is more than I thought it would be. Pulling the plants up to move them here was easy. Dig them up; put them in the sled. Replanting requires constant decisions. What would look good where or next to what other plants?

When finally I have everything in the ground, I say to Martha "Where is the spigot for the hose?"

"There isn't one."

Next I am filling up a gallon milk jug repeatedly at the kitchen sink to bless the new flowerbeds with water. Fortunately, most of the planting is right along the house. There are some curly green and white hostas around a tree next to the driveway and a nice set of deep indigo wild iris along with the blues, purples, and yellows of the rescued Johnny-jump-ups bordering a large granite slab sitting in the lawn. Finally, it's all done. I anoint myself Clean Woman with a refreshing shower.

That's when the bug bites become obvious. Usually, I'm pale white all over. Martha refers to our skin type as cheap Irish skin. I can get a sunburn on a drizzly day due to a phenomenon called refraction. It has something to do with rays of the sun bouncing off water droplets. I'm the type to wear hat, gloves, and long sleeves on a boat, so when I see these black fly bites I see bright red pocks contrasted against pale see-through skin. This is not a simple contact dermatitis. This is a reaction. They won't make me ill, but I know I'll carry these little wounds for days if not weeks. When I do a shift at the group home in Massachusetts tomorrow, I'll have to explain it is safe to be near me. I am not contagious.

Two weeks later I decide to haul some more stuff to Monroe. This time I decide to be efficient and mistakenly think I can save gas by driving with my windows open. It's warm, but not hot, and I'm pretty clever. For a few hours I drive past lawns and hayfields. Singing along with the radio because the traffic is so loud even I can't hear my off key voice, I have a nice trip until maybe an hour after I'm at the Monroe house. The trip with the garden was easy compared to what happens next. My breathing nearly shuts off. I know I should consider going to the hospital, so I consider it, and decide against it. I take my medicines, use all my inhalers, and conclude I'll be fine as long as I once again limit myself to just breathing and sleeping.

In the morning I start making some rules to guide me in my new life in my old habitat. First, I decide my health will have to be a priority. I decide my health has been a priority for the last few years and it would be more fun to focus on something else. I remember I have given up on real estate and decide Rule #1 is No More Real Estate and right away I decide Rule #2 is to Take Care of My Health. Now I'm getting somewhere.

## Once More to the Village

In Freedom Village our family's house was across the street from the rundown gray clapboard Banton Brothers Mill, down the street from the Bangs & Knight IGA store, and only a few houses away from the old post office which is now just the remnants of a granite block foundation. I grew from a child into a young woman while living in a mustard-colored colonial home which, too, has decayed and gone.

All of this is, or isn't anymore, in the village, the hub of the town of Freedom. After leaving for college in 1966, when I looked back, the place haunted me. It was where we had just moved when my mother died from heart disease in 1959 and the town I'd only recently left when my father died in 1966, from lung cancer. I had lived there with my father and brother, who left to join the Navy one week after graduating from high school. My two older sisters stayed in Massachusetts. For my last two years of high school it was simply me, the youngest, and Daddy. We weren't close. He said I was kind of uppity and constantly reminded me of how children in Ireland, where he was born in 1903, were better behaved. I'm sure children there had changed, too, but I wasn't in a position to mention it.

My move back to Maine, which feels like defeat, has me thinking back to the lonely childhood memories I have both cherished and avoided in the village that I have both loved and dreaded. Although I was grateful for the comfort of a small town, I also feared being trapped there in the place on earth where I had been the most lonely, felt the most cold. Years later my therapist described Freedom as a great misnomer in my life. I saw the town as at least that and a lot more.

The town of Freedom is still here even though some of the parts I knew best are gone. The village, the central part of town, isn't central at all. It's in the corner bordering on the town of Knox and, barely past the entrance to the pond, the town of Montville. For many years after I had grown up and moved away, I was almost afraid to enter the village. I never came back to Freedom to visit deliberately, but if I were in Maine I felt compelled to stop by my parents' graves on Knox Ridge. From there I would drive down into the town and through the village, without getting out of the car.

My fear was I would go along Route 137, hooking a left up onto what is now called Main Street, when a large plastic bubble would form over the village, sealing shut with me in it. I wouldn't even have time to backtrack to the Knox line. I'd be back in, oh maybe 1962, once again a lonely child who wanted to know the meaning of life. My father would be alive again, since in this version of the village he wouldn't have died yet.

I would wear plaid wool skirts with knee socks and live in the old house with my father and brother. We usually walked anywhere we went and we never once, as I recall, went anywhere, the three of us together. My father said he didn't own a car or drive because he was color blind. There was also no money to speak of.

Danny and I shared a blue Schwinn bike that had been our sister Jo's. We weren't good at sharing. One time when we disagreed on whose day it was, I rode the bike but he followed me everywhere. I don't have memories of being hungry or beaten. Spanked, yes, but not beaten. It wasn't that kind of physically abusive childhood. I mostly remember being lonely. I understood loneliness to be a part of me like some people are friendly, some are grumpy. I was lonely. I ached. I wanted my mother. If she'd been there, I believe the abuse that went past neglect wouldn't have happened. I have to believe that. The abuse I recall was personal, but I rarely talk about it even to myself.

When I drive through Freedom now in real time, I notice first what is no longer standing. The Banton Brothers Mill, once a thriving lumber mill on the brook across from our house, has been gone a long time. No surprise. It was falling down when we first moved to town forty-five years ago. Our house is gone, and has been for some years. Danny told me the house had collapsed within a few years after we sold it for two thousand dollars to a neighbor. On one of those quick drives through the village, I knew I'd be seeing a pile of rubble when I looked up at the house. I wondered how I would feel. Could my childhood be put away, be erased? Would I ache again? The first time I was back in Freedom after hearing of the house's collapse, I pulled up alone to the spot, looked over to the mess and let out an audible sigh of relief. *Whew, there is no way I will ever have to live there again.* At that time, I had my home and family in Massachusetts. There was no plan, no reason to think I would have to live there, but I was relieved to now have the extra layer. Not only was it not planned, it wasn't even possible.

Yet, here I am back in Maine. Now unmarried, my family grown, I'm alone again. I'm pleasantly surprised I'm not intensely lonely, but the familiar loneliness has been replaced with overwhelming disappointment. I no longer have a deep-down dread of existing in a vacuum of my own. Now I have constant inner chatter, nothing I can't interrupt to carry on a conversation with someone else, but a steady stream of lists of things I have not accomplished. I live with the weight of failure. Although I spend a lot of time alone in my rooms at Martha's, it's time I use to plan my way out of who I am now.

I occasionally check out Freedom again and sometimes I even get out of the car. I'm not a gambler, unless you call a real estate career gambling, but I do play the Maine State Lottery in Freedom. When I pass through town I usually stop into the Freedom General Store, the place I always knew as Knowlton's Garage, and spring for a two dollar scratch ticket. It would be neat to win, but much sweeter to win in Freedom. Sometimes I get enough to buy another ticket, never more than that yet, though. Not yet.

On one of my recent trips I decided to check out the pond. As kids in the village we spent a lot of summer days up there and only this past summer the place was mentioned on the Bangor TV news.

"Freedom Dam. Who owns it?"

That teaser headline gave me an amusing jolt with a flash-back. When I was growing up in Freedom, we never made the evening news. This broadcast featured a reporter doing a stand-up at the edge of Freedom Pond. To his credit, he called it that, too. Written as Sandy Pond on maps, it is Freedom Pond in real life. He described our dam as an earthen berm dam. To us, it was just the dam and it cut a line through the part of the pond we knew best. There were two good ways to get to it. The old way, only Freedom people would know, was through a dairy farm. We would cross a pasture, go through the woods, and along a path making a U turn at a slab pile. If we stuck to the path, possible only because we already knew the way, we would come out on the far side of the dam. That was good when we were not in a hurry or did not want to walk up Academy Hill. By way of the road, we would climb the hill past the burned-out foundation and chimney of Freedom Academy, past Freedom Congregational Church, past Freedom Grammar School and on towards the dam road. We liked saying dam road. It was like saying a swear word without swearing. The dam road. These days the dirt road is clearly marked as a boat launch site. Back then, in the early sixties, before the decade went tie dyed, it was simply a dirt lane.

Once we were on the dam road, we still had to cross two parallel boards running lengthwise over an outlet for the pond. In the spring, these boards spanned a raging stream but by fall, they lay over what every year became a swampy area. I was always worried the boards would not hold me up or I would lose my balance and fall in the water. Grown men crossed there, but I was frightened my weight might somehow be too much one day, that I would be the one crossing when the boards gave way. I feared those boards, but I was also afraid of all the fish in the pond and the eels, although I never saw an eel. The other kids in town told me about them, maybe hoping to see my reaction. They knew I still had a lot of city kid in me.

I always tried to take on that two-board bridge like a trooper, and nearly every time I thought I had conquered it, another kid would say something like, "What are you so afraid of? This thing's only a few feet off the ground."

I usually went up to the pond with my friend Paula, and we would swim alone or meet other kids up there. Parents did not go; lifeguards were unheard of. So, we had the place to ourselves. We would jump off the wooden platform that housed a turning device used to regulate the water level from the upper pond into the lower. The platform jutted out midway across the dam. To get to it we had to pick our way over granite boulders making up the dam's construction. We were familiar enough with each of these rocks so we took what had seemed like a path to us, even though there was no obvious route. Almost every day in summer, we crossed the two-board bridge, hit our stride on the granite boulders, and stood free. Once on the dam, there was pond on either side of us. In front, lay the pond itself, including a small island and a turn to the right, where the pond opened up into something big enough to look like a small lake. Behind us, there was the sorry lower pond, which seemed to go lower every year until it was no more than mosquito haven and standing water swamp.

In recent years, even the upper pond is lower. A few years ago in 2000, when we were all in Monroe for Thanksgiving at Martha's house, I took my kids over to Freedom to see the dam of my youth. As I plucked my way along the boulders, I looked up to see them walking easily.

"Uh, Mom. There's a path here."

In my day they would have been chest high or at least knee deep in water depending on how far along we were in the season. They were walking along a patch of grass and gravel almost big enough to be a small beach area.

"Anyway," I said. "This is it."

I know they cannot picture the times we had. They cannot imagine the Pottle boys, with their small boat, towing us each in turn on a board we used as if it were water skis. They cannot picture me swimming out to the island to see if I could make it. It is not far, but swimming was the only thing I ever flunked in my life. They did not ask me who owned the dam. They accepted from me it was the dam in town.

I do not know who owns it now, but I know we acted as if we owned it then, in the manner of eminent domain. The kids in town staked our claim and made good on it by uninterrupted use. The town, I expect, will one day come to own the dam in order to maintain it. The news story was prompted by a concern that if the dam were breached, the town of Freedom would be flooded out. There is still enough room for water in the lower pond before Freedom Village gets drenched, but overall, maintaining the dam is no doubt a good idea. It still has the capacity for making many more memories. It's one of the places that prompts me to try to reconcile the difference between what I am now with what I thought I'd be when I was still growing up.

When it wasn't swimming season, I used to sit alone at the dam. Sometimes I would sit and read, sometimes I would sit and think, and sometimes I would plan my future. I wanted to be an actress, but not a model; I knew I would want a speaking part in life. I did consider joining the June Taylor Dancers, the ones on the Jackie Gleason Show. I also decided to be a doctor, well maybe, if I could have a career in research and cure something. At some point I settled on travel journalist.

I wanted to be famous, not because I wanted a lot of attention; but because I equated fame with respect. I wanted people to know I was something, that I had done something well. As a young person I had a lot of plans, but as an adult, one day Lily Tomlin wrapped it up for me when I heard her say, "I always wanted to be somebody, but now I realize I should have been more specific."

Being whatever I am now was never in my plans.

\*     \*     \*     \*     \*

Now in June 2004 Martha and I decide to go to the Dirigo Grange Hall in Freedom Village for the Strawberry Festival. It's a chicken pot pie supper followed by all the strawberry shortcake you can eat. We pull up at the Grange Hall which sits at the point of a triangle where High Street merges into Route 137. Cars are lined up, more than I have ever seen here before.

We casually follow others into the back door of the Grange and as we are paying our six dollars each, I look around the room. Didn't expect my knees to buckle, didn't expect to feel so faint. The patterned tin ceiling painted light green extends halfway down the wall to wainscoting. I never noticed that as a kid. The stage, at the opposite end of the room is no higher than a few steps up. I'm sure that's the way it was, even if not the way I remember it.

So much of the Freedom I knew is gone or changed, but now I am in the upper level of the Grange Hall and the memories wash over me. Here is where we had town hall meetings, dances, and the occasional traveling show. One time, in this very room, I danced with my father. I don't remember what event it was or exactly why he was there since he rarely went to anything. He asked me to dance and I said yes, right here on these floor boards. It was a quiet, public pleasantry lasting a few minutes and then a lifetime.

Tonight's Strawberry Festival goers are seated around the perimeter of the room waiting for the second seating. Second seating, in the Grange Hall. I love it. I don't recognize anyone in the town where I once knew everyone. Why would I? I'm not wearing a plaid wool skirt; they're not wearing dark green Dickies work trousers. My remembered version of the town stood still, but the actual town did not. When we are told they are ready for us downstairs, people head down a staircase that was never there before. I always remember going up and down a narrow stairway twisting around the back of the stage, but we are heading down wide straight stairs leading to the lower Grange Hall. I get my first glimpse of the old dining area, newly knotty pined.

The supper is fantastic. We are seated family style at long tables. Everyone is friendly and people keep coming around to ask, "Do you want some more?" "Do you have enough cream?" We eat home style chicken pot pies, drink lemonade and coffee, before beginning on the strawberries. There are a few bowls of whole berries on each table. Each diner scoops some into their own bowl and slices them using a round biscuit cutter, much like a cookie cutter only with a taller handle. Martha and I, along with everyone else I assume, eat plenty.

"I'm full. Are you full?"

"Are you kidding? I'm beyond full."

That's all the conversation we could muster as we walk, although it feels like waddling, back out to the car. We laugh at ourselves and agree it was a good time.

On the way back to Monroe we spot a double rainbow over the Camden Hills. I pull over and quickly grab my digital camera from the back seat to capture this beauty, this moment. I decide to cap off a great evening with a great shot.

The next day I see I should have taken "cap off" more literally as in - take the lens cap off. I remind myself it doesn't matter. Even if not in photos, memories are captured. It's time for me to make some new ones.

# Retreat

It's nice living in the country where I can walk among my gardens in the morning, with a cup of coffee in hand. It's nice but not necessarily productive. There is the matter of my car payment, trying to pay Martha some rent money, plus the simple joys of life like gas and groceries. I have come home to write, hoping I will be able to find a way to support myself while I try.

Things are going well because I'm in the right place to do some unwinding. I feel like a phone cord, twisted so much it has lost its reach even though it can still work. It does what it has to do, but it isn't pretty and it isn't easy to use. With one pull in any direction, the cord I am can bring the phone crashing down to the floor, or knocking over my coffee, or landing on my foot, or any of those things. All of those things. That's how I feel. It doesn't matter though, how I feel. I still have to work; I still have to work through my feelings.

People who know I have to deal with illness seem to be aware of the breast cancer, or the asthma or a combination of the two, but my most debilitating illness is depression. When I was being treated for cancer, I learned the difference between being tired and having fatigue. Tired is easy. The solution is getting some rest. Fatigue is still there despite getting rest, it permeates so even small tasks demand a big effort. Being unhappy is like being tired, but depression has the strength, the longevity of fatigue. I can laugh at a joke, have a good time with some friends then, even while I'm still with them, detach from the situation wishing I could be one of them. Anyone walking by would not notice me as anything but one of the group. In the time it takes for a thought, my mood can plummet from laughing with friends to realizing I'm not happy, no sense pretending. Although I've been treated for anxiety as well, I like to think my anxiety days are over. Still I do feel like a twisted phone cord, so who am I kidding? Once the depression has hold of me, anxiety is easily next in line. A solid bout of depression can cancel out my anxiety replacing it with what feels like fatigue. Depression makes me feel heavy, but has nothing to do with my weight.

June and July of this year are turning out to be busy months for me, if you can call driving up and down the Maine Turnpike busy. I'm still picking up hours at the group home, although I know I'll have to quit that job. It doesn't pay enough to warrant the mileage. I do need new work, but I have one more place to go first.

Among the favorite things in my life is the Women's Writing Retreat I attend every July in the Adirondacks. Including a storytelling weekend at the same center, this trip will have me away for about ten days. It seems frivolous to be going on vacation when I barely work, but I've backed out of my former life to unwind. There is no better place for me to be during the week of the retreat. Knowing I could not stand to be anywhere that week if I could not be there, I decide to keep my plans made months ago. My first year there was 1996, right before my initial cancer diagnosis. This is my ninth time attending; I'm not giving up this treat this year.

The site is about eight hundred acres of Adirondack paradise near Fort Ticonderoga in upstate New York, not far from the Vermont border. There is a lake with only the retreat center on its shore. It's an eight-hour drive from Monroe whether I go across Maine through the mountains or go down the coast and diagonally across New Hampshire and Vermont. I've never taken the route across Maine because I've never left for the retreat from Waldo County before. It still isn't an option this time because my third summer I brought along my friend Margaret Kelly. We always travel there together now. She lives back in the Amesbury area, so I head towards Massachusetts spending the first night of the trip in my old room at Matt's house in Kittery. When daylight comes indoors, I wake up realizing I have once again come to my favorite day of the year. Grabbing the few things I brought in for the night, I quickly head further south to pick up Margaret, stopping only at a bagel shop to get my own breakfast and some pastry for a gift.

Because I have moved to Maine, I don't see my Massachusetts people, friends and family as often as I might like. One of those people is my Aunt Catherine. Except for my three older siblings, she is my only living elder. There are some relatives in Ireland and England, and there is her cousin Michael who lives next door to her, but she is the only one I answer to. Aunt Catherine has lived her whole life in Lowell, Massachusetts, the first sixty something years in the same house where she and my mother grew up, the last twenty-five years in her newer house, a small one-level home on the better side of town. Both houses happen to be numbered 102.

When I mentioned this to her once she simply said, "Yes, that's right." Nothing more.

I haven't seen her for a few months. Margaret and I will be going through Lowell on Route 495, so I take this opportunity to stop in with a few scones. Not sure it will be an opportunity, but it is a chance to visit without making a special trip. As soon as I knew I'd be moving to Maine, I told my aunt so she couldn't accuse me of not telling her. She asked, "Do you have a job up there?"

I admitted I didn't yet. "Oh . . . like your mother." My mother moved to Maine in 1958 and died three months later. She was fifty-six years old. I'll be fifty-six this summer.

Sitting on her sofa like two proper children, Margaret and I make nice talk. We sip tea and say we do have a long ride ahead of us. Catherine became pleased I go to this place in the Adirondacks when I told her it is owned by the Roman Catholic Diocese of Albany. I know it does not adhere to Aunt Catherine's strict sense of being Roman Catholic. She is a patroness of the Poor Clares, a cloistered community of women who have given over their lives to prayer. The nuns I know at the retreat center wear shorts and T shirts and are there as, well, people who are there.

"You look like the Bobsey twins," Catherine tells us. Margaret and I turn to look at each other; we are both wearing turquoise shirts. Hers has a white collar; mine is a T shirt with a white wavy stripe. We might have driven all the way to Canada and back without noticing this, but now we sit two Bobseys on a sofa.

Once I am backing out of my aunt's driveway in retreat, I feel I am covered now for six to eight weeks before I will sense I should make contact again. I am still trying to talk myself past whatever verbal acupuncture my aunt has delivered when Margaret says, "I think she's nice. You look alike, I can see you're related."

"Nice," I say. If it were possible to quadruple all the hugs I got from family members, maybe we could come close to a warm, loving family.

"She loves you."

"She does," I admit. Like most of the people who have loved me, it is correct to say she does. It is also correct to say she doesn't do it well. Even my husband hadn't done it very well and I picked him.

"That's family," I say. "You get what you get."

Margaret got an even more disjointed family so we could talk about this for hours, but we don't. We are moving on, moving forward to retreat.

Heading out across Massachusetts on Route 2, also known as the Mohawk Trail, we go up and down hills and small mountains, follow alongside rivers and always, always making time for coffee breaks. It's our first time taking this particular road, an old Native American trade route. Members of the Five Nations traveled this way between the Connecticut River Valley in what is now Massachusetts and the Hudson River Valley in upstate New York. We stop almost into North Adams at The Western Summit where there is an observation point, a small gift shop, and one of the most remarkable views in New England. This area has been known as Spirit Mountain by the local Native Americans and the view alone could warrant the name. We are treated to lush green layers of land culminating in a view of local mountains including Mount Greylock, the highest point in Massachusetts. We have ascended to a great height on our way to a place that gives us an annual high. Overlooking these green rolling hills, we are swept with awe. We like to collect views on these long rides, but no matter which of the roads we are on, often I won't stop to look at them because I'm so excited about getting to the retreat. We usually point, say "View!"

and keep going, but his particular sight is incredible so we get out of the car to look with great appreciation before we continue. As much as we are charmed though, we are becoming increasingly excited about getting where we are going. We don't want to linger. We are quickly back in the car and on our way again.

Margaret is easy to please, she seems to appreciate everything. I first met her when I started my part-time group home career, back in 1995. She seemed like a nice person but not one particularly literate. She is actually a very nice person submerged in a lack of confidence due to a raging case of dyslexia. Over the years we have become good friends, such good friends there is a rumor at the retreat that we are a couple. Sorry to disappoint, but we are good friends. We usually get our own little cabin, not because we so much want to be together but because we want our own bathroom and a quiet night. The bigger cabins have shared bathrooms. Our choice has more to do with middle age incontinence than romance.

The retreat is always magic, more community than competition. The peaceful setting along with the wonderful company of writing women remains an annual personal renewal. Some years I show up as a twisted phone cord and other years, pen in hand, I'm ready to work. In July of 1999 I found out for sure on a Friday I did, indeed, have cancer again. I was at the retreat two days later and spent most of the week sitting on a large boulder overlooking the lake, writing in a journal, and listening to the loons. I was sitting as I used to sit at Freedom Pond. I did manage to squeeze out a few poems that year. Most of my finished writing wasn't memorable, but the process was worthwhile.

Once we get to Paradox, NY, we look for the dirt road that takes us to the lake. The Pyramid Life Center is the only thing on the road, at the very end. On our way in, we spot a deer. My first year at the retreat, I woke up to a rustling noise outside my window. Fortunately, I sat up in time to see a deer munching before it casually walked off. Yesterday leaving Monroe I saw a doe and fawn at the opening to a woods road. They stood so still I thought they might be statues, fake deer, but the mother moved and the baby followed. Now a deer has come to greet us before we go into the dining hall to check in.

This year I'm here on a Friday for the weekend storytelling workshop offered before the actual writing retreat running from Sunday through Friday. Unlike the Women's Writing Retreat, this group is both men and women. As we all gather in the boat house on the first night, we do the round of introductions, telling a little bit about ourselves including where we are from.

"I'm Ellie O'Leary. I live in Monroe, Maine. I've done this workshop a few times before and . . ."

I hear one of the facilitators say, "That didn't used to be true. Did it? You lived in Massachusetts."

He's right and he knows it. He lives in Massachusetts and remembers I did, too. This year is different though. This year I am reinventing myself.

Storytelling is a funny thing for me. Apparently, I do it fairly well, but it isn't a strong interest of mine. I never get into the fairy tale sort of stories; I prefer the personal tales. For my effort I do a short piece about a little girl lost in the woods, telling myself it isn't autobiographical. I'm lucky enough to have a prop; for the girl's heartbeat I use my tap shoes. I usually have them with me for the retreat because I tap every year to the camp song known as *The Peanut Butter Jail.*

For the last few years I have been on the organizing committee for the retreat and have been the emcee every evening for the readings. It's totally volunteer. I seem to be good at the jobs that pay little or nothing. As much as I loved doing all that, it became too much this past spring along with nearly everything else. I had driven all the way to Albany one Sunday for a committee meeting where we each passed the "talking stick". As the stick was handed to each of us, it was our turn to speak. We had already started the meeting, but the one with the talking stick showed up a little bit late and we had to start all over, using the stick, to accommodate her. The next day I had a message on my real estate voice mail from the same woman. She said she and I still had something to settle. I'll never know what it was. I had said, the day before, I volunteered out of a position of gratitude. A day later she still wanted to settle something. I already had lots to settle with myself so within a few days, I resigned from the committee. Now I'm here without the responsibility I had in previous recent years. I wondered how it would feel to be in my new role or my lack of a role. Like so many things this year, it feels surprisingly good to let go. My sense of being a telephone cord is untangling some more.

Having fun here is a natural. We gather every year, a lot of the same women, and every year some new ones. I feel fortunate not only to share the place with Margaret, but also with my two favorite redheads, my daughter Brigid and Matt's girlfriend Gretyl. The kids come in their own wheels and stay together in the same cabin, where they are assigned. There's going to the place where your mother goes and there's actually going with your mother. Gretyl's mother is here too, having traveled with someone from her area.

One of my favorite women of all time is Mooncat, not her real name, who teaches fiction. Everyone here calls her Mooncat; a few of the women use nicknames in this place. Mooncat calls me Tapcat. She writes mysteries, the most recent of which is set in a retirement community based on the one where she lives in Maryland. An outrageous older woman, it says so on a T shirt she sometimes wears, Mooncat is an octogenarian I'm proud to know. I have learned a lot from her, both on writing and on things in general. I once told her I wish she were my mother; she replied she wished I were her daughter. I didn't mean instead of my mother, any more than she meant instead of the daughter she already has. We were sort of wishing, adding to our lives.

For my two chosen workshops this week, I'm doing fiction with Mooncat and poetry with Julie, another long-time presenter here. The poetry is haiku leading into tanka. I make a solid effort writing a few haiku about rain, pine trees, lightning but I'm not looking to tighten my writing. I'm trying to get it up and spit it out. Julie always teaches more than the form by itself so I am taken with the idea of the haiku moment, the burst causing you to feel nature intensely then to write about it tightly with a twist, in only seventeen syllables. She tells us the way to experience this is to go on a journey walk or monk's walk, a quiet meditative stroll. So I go for a walk; that much I can do.

Mornings here are in workshops and afternoons are open to possibilities. There are hiking trails, swimming, canoes and kayaks, and one of my favorite afternoon activities – a good old-fashioned nap. Ever since the first time I had cancer, I've never been quite healthy again. I have never fully regained the energy I once had. Naps are part of my schedule.

All of our meals are buffet style in the central dining hall. On the wall there is a big wooden sign with the words of a blessing sung to the tune of Edelweiss. This is the only place where I sing out loud anywhere near other people. I figure if you are simply trying to say thank you, you don't have to be on key.

Brigid is another person I don't see nearly as often as I would like. My daughter lives in Belchertown in western Massachusetts and works two jobs, one she likes and one she loves. Her job at the local Whole Foods is okay, but her real passion is to coach figure skating. She has skated since she was three and picked her original college, York University in Toronto, because of the skating program. When the school shut down on strike her first semester, she came home disillusioned. I am proud of how she has made her own way in a part of the state where we knew nobody. She moved out west, as I call it, with friends and took some courses at a community college. Last year she drove the hour and a half to my house in Amesbury to tell me she wanted to drop out of college to coach skating. She thought I would be upset, but I am more in the do-what-you-love camp.

I'm happy she is here, that she's passionate about everything creative and holistic. It turns out her name has been a good choice; she wears it well. When some of the more touchy-feely crowd here explain about the myths, legends and goddesses, especially in the Celtic realm, we get a good laugh. I'm sometimes viewed as too business-like to be into such stuff, but I did name my daughter after the patroness saint of Ireland, didn't I? Most Irish saints, and there are hundreds of them, come from pre-Christian legends. St. Brigid is among them.

Brigie and I sit by the lake having a mother-daughter talk, inevitable even on retreat. She lives with her boyfriend and to me he is a drain on her resources. It breaks my heart to see her give so much of herself to someone who offers so little in return. It's not that I don't like him at all, but I wish he were not her boyfriend. The strain between us is real, but at least it is confined only to this topic. Brigid has a new car I am seeing for the first time, a red Ford Focus. I bought her a red dust brush because I know she will be thrilled to keep her vehicle looking great.

By Thursday night we have all been refreshed with each other's company, new people are forever altered in a good way, and it's almost time to say goodbye. Almost. The last night is the time for the closing ritual. We have over the years developed a few things that were never planned; those are the elements that endure. One year the whole place was overrun by mice and Sister Monica, who runs Pyramid Life Center, came up with a way to trap them with peanut butter. One of the women writers put together a ditty to the tune of *Charlie on the MTA*, called it *The Peanut Butter Jail*, and we had our camp song. Even I'm not sure how it came about I would dance to it, but we have our fun. Also on Thursday night, our shawls come out. We never decided this as I recall; it somehow came about. Women started wearing shawls of all sorts over their shoulders, particularly if they were doing a reading that final night. Depending on who is on the committee in any given year the ritual can vary, but the one component that matters most is the fire circle between the boathouse and the lake. By the end of this final night we are enjoying the bonfire as we sing, make s'mores, and tell stories. We say goodbye, though we have one more workshop in the morning, and we will all say goodbye again by lunch time.

Goodbye for me this year means I have to come down from the magic mountain, to go back to the mess of my life. I have told people here I quit my job to go home to Maine to write, but that is a real glossing-over of the fact I am lonely, broke, and severely disappointed with myself. My hope is maybe the challenge of pulling out of my emotional, physical, and financial problems will at least hold my interest long enough for me to get some writing done.

I have moved home to Maine with a new job after all, but the big detail I have to work around is that the job is in Massachusetts. For the last few years I have volunteered as a guest speaker at a first time homebuyer workshop. The last time I spoke I told the woman who coordinates it that she will need a new real estate agent to speak, but she surprised me by saying she is looking for someone to take charge of the workshop. My first question is, "It's not volunteer, is it?"

Volunteering to speak occasionally is one thing, but taking responsibility for the whole thing without pay would be something else entirely.

"No, you would be paid as an independent contractor. A consultant."

Well, doesn't sound good to me! A consultant. I like the name of the job. The bulk of the tasks, handling inquiries and registrations, is done by phone, fax, and email. It doesn't matter where I live as long as I show up when an actual workshop is scheduled - which means four trips to Massachusetts for four consecutive weeks about every other month.

Sometimes I find myself singing my new favorite song adapted from *Jesus Christ Superstar*, "Always Hoped That I'd be a Consultant, Knew that I could make it if ......" well, if I screwed up my old job enough. I love being a consultant; I try to be honest about it. I don't want to work nine to five. I do not want to be on call 24/7 or anything close to the schedule required of a real estate agent. I don't have the physical or emotional energy to work full-time, so I'm a consultant because right now it fits. I sometimes refer to myself as semi-retired. I love it when someone else tells me they are a consultant. I want to ask, "So did you get fired or quit? Laid off, maybe?" I don't ask though. That's not the way we were raised in Waldo County. Here anyone else's business is pretty much none of mine, unless they need some help. Even then it's generally inappropriate to ask personal questions.

Now back from the retreat I begin working on the homebuyer's workshop, the first one I will be facilitating myself. It will be near the end of August, so I've got to get busy scheduling guest speakers including an agent, a home inspector, and loan originator.

First I feel compelled to celebrate, or at least acknowledge, my birthday at the beginning of the month. My two friends back in Amesbury, Cathy and Carol, have been able to help me get through a lot. We used to get together one morning a week calling ourselves the Breakfast Club and they ran the Ellie O'Leary Cancer Relief Fund that helped so much in 1999 after my second diagnosis. Right on my birthday the mail brings a card from Carol that includes a campaign style pin. It's bright yellow with black uneven writing made to look like it was scrawled by hand. **"I survived damn near everything!"** Oh, I survived. Good news. I laugh and cry at the pin and feel good somebody thinks of me as a survivor and not a loser.

Because today, August 6, is my birthday, I go over all of everything about myself from the beginning. My real name is Helen Jane O'Leary. I'm named after my mother Helen Frances Mary Healey O'Leary. Mary was her confirmation name and it is mine as well, but in a generational difference she used it as a part of her name and I never do. Here in Waldo County people I already know, from way back when, call me Helen; people I meet call me Ellie.

When anyone asks me how I got Ellie from Helen, I give the simple and true answer that I picked it. In 1986 we had newly moved to Amesbury so I had a good chance to start over. I was in therapy for depression and looking for some relief.

As a kid I sometimes heard "Helen is dead," but I was alive. Occasionally when I visited my Aunt Catherine in the summer, someone would say "Doesn't she look like Helen?"

I wanted to jump up saying, "I don't look like Helen. I am Helen." I was polite and quiet, crying only inside myself or when I was alone. I was sure girls with mothers cried to their mothers or didn't cry much at all. In Freedom no one knew my mother well, since she died a few months after we moved there. Most people in town hadn't ever met her, so my mind took the opportunity to make her up and, in the process, elevate her to Saint Helen. I believed had she lived everything, and I mean everything, would have been better. I figured out for myself back then, and therefore truly believed, girls with mothers didn't have problems.

My mother was born in 1902 when Helen was a lovely, common name for a baby girl much like the names Susan or Linda in my age group. Her mother, Ellen Daly Healey, died when my mother was a little girl. My mother must have liked being named with a variation of her mother's name since she carried on the practice. I wanted to use Junior, Helen O'Leary, Jr., like my brother, Daniel Joseph O'Leary, Jr. I was told girls were not allowed to do that.

I liked being named after my mother when she was alive. Once she wasn't, the name was a dead weight. Every day when the school bus took me to Mount View High School, after it took a left on top of Knox Ridge, I'd look over to the small cemetery to see my name on a gravestone. First I would remind myself my mother was dead, and then I'd go to normal high school things like gym class, algebra, and student council.

My two older sisters are named Barbara and Josephine, but for some reason my parents waited until me to give a daughter our mother's name. Within the family I was usually called Honey, a nickname my brother gave me when he was a toddler and I was an infant. I asked my father if they named me Helen because they couldn't think of anything once they got their fourth and final child. He said no, they wanted it that way and seemed at least a bit surprised by the question. I felt extra, as if the family had not lasted long enough to finish raising me. My father, my brother, and I each courted our own memories and wishes. We were living individually, not as a family.

As an adult I realized being whoever I wanted to be included choosing my own name. Coming out from under a dead woman's name helped me. I became known as Ellie, although I did not change my name legally. I wasn't rejecting my mother. Though I didn't want to use it, I had been given my mother's name. How could I in good conscience give it up entirely?

To at least acknowledge, if not celebrate, my birthday today, I have decided to take a long ride to someplace - almost any place. Living here as a kid, of course I saw the coast, but I saw a lot more of the woods. Today I decide to explore some coastline. If I head south I'll be in Camden, a good place to spend money, but not what I am about these days. I decide to head north which, as Mainers know, will actually take me Down East.

My road trip goes across the Waldo-Hancock Bridge, over the Penobscot River, to the north side of Penobscot Bay. I notice the scenery now that I'm back. The large, inhabited islands in the expanse of the sparkling waters of the bay, provide views that cause tourists to rave. As a young local, I barely noticed such things. As an older local, fifty-six today, the woods to the water's edge and the clusters of moored sailboats make me glad I'm home. I'm not happy I'm back broke and lonely, but on my birthday I'll take in some views if I want.

The day goes well including lunch in Blue Hill. I get a great sandwich on crusty French bread and decide to eat it on the town pier. There are two young children fishing with their grandmother. She is showing each kid how to cast their lines; they've found a great way to spend a summer day. They don't strike me as summer people, but real Down Easters. I'm not into fishing but a day at the pier with a grandparent looks like a good day to me.

My own day is a decent balance of reflection and action. Driving alone can cause me to be too inward, but today I'm driving for the pleasure of it, not to get somewhere by a certain time. After being able to treat myself to such a relaxing day, maybe there's hope I'll be okay after all.

A few weeks later Martha and I go to the Marsh River Theatre in Brooks to hear the River City Harmonizers singing show tunes and old ballads. Well, I go to hear them. Martha is one of them. I'm happy for her that she has this group of singing women. They practice once a week and have become more than a musical group to each other. It's a nice summer evening and all is well.

The next morning I get a phone call from my sister Jo.

"Honey?"

"Yeah."

"It's Aunt Catherine. She died in her sleep. Not last night, the night before."

"Oh." My aunt had been found dead at home from her heart condition on the morning of the evening I was enjoying the concert.

"They didn't have your phone number, so they called me."

I'm the only one of my siblings who kept in touch with Aunt Catherine consistently over the last forty years. Barbara sometimes sent her holiday greeting cards for Christmas and St. Patrick's Day, Danny ignored her, and Josephine reconnected within the last two years after decades of silence.

"They couldn't find my phone number? Who are *they*?"

I know Aunt Catherine has kept every slip of paper that matters nicely organized in her polished mahogany secretary. I don't know why anyone would be able to find one sister's phone number, but not the other. Josephine tells me friends tried to bring my aunt some home cooked food on Saturday morning but, when she did not answer, they went next door to her cousin Michael's house. He entered using the key she had given him for this sort of occasion. Although she was there in her bed, she was gone. She was ninety-two years old.

A few days later at the funeral home, my aunt is laid out in the same room where a decade before, her husband Bernard had been, and a decade before that, her Aunt Mary. I remember standing there with her in front of Bern's casket at his wake when she said to me, "Doesn't he look good?"

"He does," I said out loud as I thought, *What difference does it make what he looks like? He is definitely dead.*

After Aunt Mary's funeral Mass, she told me, "You did well. You know your responses."

"My mother taught me."

I used the opportunity to put in a plug for the elder Helen who had taken me to many a Mass where I learned to respond correctly to the priest. Catherine saw it as religious and I saw it as a classic psychological stimulus-response reaction. I couldn't recite the Mass, but if the priest says his part, I know mine.

Neither of us mentioned the major detail that I was not raised Catholic. My family, since way before me, had been Catholic but (the way my father explained it) my mother had a falling out with the Pope. We were raised High Episcopal. She apparently didn't believe in infallibility and died before I knew what that was.

My aunt had over the years described my mother with terms such as *bold* in a way that *bold* was not good. I heard how that Helen had embarrassed the family by getting her hair bobbed. Such stories didn't caution me to be good, but made me wish I had gotten to know that Helen with the courage to have short hair.

Today at the funeral home, the letters on the felt board spell Katherine McArdle. That won't do. Another relative tells me when she called the funeral home to see if they needed an obituary, they told her Mrs. McArdle had updated her own two weeks ago. When I tell the man at the desk Catherine is spelled wrong, he tells me they have had four Katherines so far this week, one of them his own mother. I explain *this* Catherine was a schoolteacher and would want her name spelled correctly. He doesn't change it right away, but Jo prompts him one more time and it is done.

The wake and funeral are taking place in Lowell, so I am spending the night in between the two at Matt's house again. On the way there, I stop in Walmart to buy a black skirt. Aunt Catherine had a great sense of the appropriate as in what is appropriate to wear to a funeral. Navy blue --- maybe, dark red --- if you must, but beige is inappropriate. I have a beige dress with me to wear but decide I don't want to take any chances in case she can see me. She may be gone, but she is still a voice in the back of my head.

For the funeral Matt and I meet Brigid in Amesbury and we all go to Lowell together in her new, bright red car. Not exactly funeral color, but she can't stop in Walmart to buy a new one. She wants to be the one to drive in the funeral procession, so we're off. I am a little bothered Luke doesn't get the day off from work, but I get over it.

This is one of those rare occasions when the four siblings of my family are together. We gather initially at the funeral home for the final viewing. When the undertaker asks all but the immediate family to leave, my brother Danny asks my kids "What about the non-immediate family?" They think their Uncle Dan is funny. I take a moment at Catherine's side, make the sign of the cross, and say thank you. Blessing myself again as I rise from the kneeler, I look at her one last time. She was bold too, in her own good way. She had character and she shared that with me.

In the parking lot the man in the black suit lines up the cars according to a list, probably proposed by my aunt when she sent in her obituary. We go together through the streets of Lowell, leaving the old Sacred Heart neighborhood where she and my mother grew up to the Immaculate Conception, the church my aunt has attended since her move in 1977. There I wonder for my brother what it must be like to have a song with your name in it played at every one of these funerals. *Oh, Danny Boy, the saints, the saints are calling.* This funeral is, of course, a Catholic Mass not a funeral ceremony. Catherine Jordan Healey McArdle had earned that. The priest mentions she led a good Christian life, but I know she would have said a good Catholic life. I make sure to get the responses right.

The post funeral luncheon is at my aunt's favorite restaurant, the same place where she had her husband's funeral gathering. I take the opportunity to visit with my sister Barbara and her daughter, Maureen, as well as my brother and his wife Judie. Josephine, who swears she is doing well now, is sometimes whispering and sometimes too loud. She promises to leave her five Yorkshire Terriers to her niece, Brigid, who looks to me for help. I don't catch all Jo is saying and tell Brigie we will deal with it later. We say our goodbyes outside the restaurant where Ronnie, Jo's husband, says she has not been doing so well. That's how we usually refer to her drinking, in euphemisms. *Josephine has not been doing well. Jo has been at it again.* Some evenings she leaves a few messages on the answering machine in Monroe, each one less intelligible than the previous. The drinking has continued and possibly escalated. I wonder when the four of us will be together again.

Back in Brigid's car, I ruminate on the past few months. My move, my aunt's death, all of it is too much. After a day of three siblings and a funeral, I feel overwhelmed, exhausted, and yet hopeful. I tell my kids Aunt Catherine's death is the end of an era in our family. I tell myself to keep going, to keep searching for whatever it is I'm missing.

# Situations

It's a Saturday back in Waldo County, a beautiful fall day when I don't have to be anywhere. That's true for most weekdays too, but on weekends I feel less awkward about it. After taking the rubbish to the transfer station I decide to go riding around. I'm going to drive down the Bog Road, mainly because B-O-G are my daughter's initials. All three kids have O'Leary for their middle name then their dad's last name, which I no longer use. This is not a road I know, but it might go to Brooks or Frankfort. I'm pretty sure I'll get lost but will eventually find my way to something I recognize – a house, a route number, a view. On these jaunts I get nostalgic comparing myself now to who I was when I left this area in 1966.

I was healthy and now I'm back, taking ten prescription medications for at least six diseases or conditions in varying states of activity. I call them my situations and believe they play games with each other behind the scenes. For Graves' Disease (a type of overactive thyroid), I no longer take medication because my thyroid seems to be doing okay on its own. For allergy induced asthma, I take four medications, recognizing the importance of breathing.

Brigid is my child most susceptible to one of the worst of my medical situations. I feel bad about bringing breast cancer into our family, but I am able to know it was no choice or negligence on my part. I remind myself there is no reason for me to feel guilty or ashamed. Breast cancer is something I can publicly claim with pride wearing a pink badge of courage, not to mention all the breast cancer T shirts, hats, and key chains. For this situation I hear people telling me I must be SO brave.

I also get one of my least favorite comments: "You're a strong person. You'll beat it." That doesn't land on me as encouragement. It's an attempt for the speaker to distance herself as in, *Thank God you're strong, so, I don't have to do anything.* Worse, it makes me think of my fellow breast cancer patients, the ones who actually died. What is the speaker saying? They were weak? People may not mean it that way, but they should consider what they are saying.

Eight years ago, I was diagnosed with Stage 2 estrogen positive breast cancer along with some DCIS, ductal carcinoma in situ. That's a cancerous, some say precancerous, condition typed as Stage 0. The treatment included surgery to remove the lump - then another surgery to establish clean margins followed by chemotherapy, radiation, and finally more chemo. It was nine months of nausea, fatigue, and confusion. Before it was finished my marriage was over. I evolved further into the constantly struggling, questioning independent I am. Whatever I might have questioned about myself before, I started to gnaw over and over. How can I make it? What's wrong with me that I can't handle everything? When the initial treatment phase finally ended, I took Tamoxifen to prevent a recurrence. Prevent is apparently too strong a term. Nothing definitely prevents a recurrence. Breast cancer has no five-year remission status. Once you've had it, as time goes by, statistically you are more likely to get it again. Three years after the cancer was first identified, I was diagnosed a second time with Stage 1 and some more DCIS. I had a mastectomy with reconstruction. I tell people my left one is a rebuilt.

My thought is, if you have to have an oncologist, try to get one with a sense of humor. I'm grateful for mine who told me, when he originally started me on chemotherapy, it wouldn't make me too nauseous.

"Some people throw up a lot on this combination" he admitted, "but they're the ones who get sick when the elevator stops."

After the second diagnosis he told me, "You did everything we asked you to do the first time. You had the surgeries, the chemo, and the radiation. There is absolutely no reason for you to be in this situation except you do have cancer again."

The good news, if you believe in silver linings, is I stopped taking Tamoxifen. With all its side effects resembling intense menopause, it wasn't missed. I was put on Arimidex, more powerful but also more pleasant, even though at first I was a bit shaken when I heard what I was being prescribed. A former co-worker taking Arimidex for metastatic breast cancer had died a few months earlier.

Being brave isn't something that enters into all this for me. I put one foot in front of the other to keep going. Self-care for breast cancer seems so black and white. I show up for appointments twice a year with my surgeon and twice a year with my oncologist. I take the medication and have an annual mammogram. Sometimes I do wear pink to show my breast cancer pride or because I have clothes I like - that happen to be pink.

Self-care for my depression, by contrast, is all shades of gray and blue. There are days when I want to wear a blue T shirt printed with "I support depression." All my medical situations have varying effects, not only on me, but also on the people around me. Each seems to get its own bundle of responses. It's alright to have osteoarthritis or asthma. Responses are neutral. If I mention I have arthritis in my knees, nobody blames me. Nobody says, "Are you sure?" It's the same thing with asthma. People don't roll their eyes or suggest I am overreacting when I go into a sneezing, coughing fit. I have three inhalers and don't need a glass of water, but when they offer one, I know they are trying to be helpful. They never make cruel jokes saying I must be off my asthma meds.

There are medications for depression and I take some of those too but, like Tamoxifen didn't prevent another bout of cancer, these don't prevent another bout of depression. They can make the bouts less frequent or less severe, but again prevent is too strong a term. People sometimes have well-meaning advice for this situation but going out for a day of fun is no more a cure for depression than eating a healthy meal is a cure for diabetes. People who wouldn't say to a diabetic "What do you mean you can't eat sugar? Lots of people eat sugar." act perfectly justified in trying to help someone dismiss their depression. I have a coffee mug that says Snap Out of It. Sometimes I like to drink from that and wear blue. Sardonic days are part of my self-care.

I know what I have. I know to stare right back at it, hands on hips, when it tries to pull me into a downward spiral. Even knowing that isn't enough every time. My depression isn't always where I can get a good look at it. It doesn't always have a precipitating event. More often depression has been attacking from within, insidiously, and eventually has me looking downward into the dark blue abyss before I know what has hold of me. Once I acknowledge I'm going through another episode, that this particular one of my situations has encroached upon my life again, I can start to defend and rebuild myself. The realization alone is helpful; it's a move towards recovery. I remind myself to go easy and not get caught up in negative internal chatter. It's no cure, but it is a strong tool. Writing also helps. For some reason I start spouting poetry at these times, not necessarily good poetry, but helpful poetry.

Today at the end of the Bog Road I have to decide either right or left. Brooks would be to my left and I know that area better so I turn right, thinking of the poet Robert Frost taking the road less traveled. It's a small decision to make; hopefully it will work out today. If not, I could always turn back, but I won't.

The pavement turns to gravel and I notice there are no power lines running along the side of the road. Okay. I'm in the country now. No buildings, no road signs, no constructed landmarks. There are no expansive views; the road is a slice through the woods. Again, my thoughts spiral down and inward.

I wonder how I once had so much ahead of me, but now I have returned — an abject failure. How could I be someone with nothing? Does that mean I'm no one?

My kids must be so embarrassed by me. They never make excuses about me, they say they're proud, but how could they be? I'm the mother who left town owing money. I'm the one who can't take care of myself. Matt's even helped me pay my car loan. I cost him money.

I left here with so much ahead of me, so much promise. I want to believe I came back older and wiser. I am a lot older, but I only have a bachelor's degree, never had a high-powered corporate job, never published a book, or was a world-renowned expert on anything. Don't own any land, never won an award, and have no equity. Success is an achievement I never reached. I wanted it, but must not have tried hard enough.

I once decided to be a world traveler, but haven't traveled nearly as much or as often as I expected or hoped. I have been to Israel and to Europe, especially Ireland, but feel as though I've never been anywhere. In Ireland people ask me directions as if I never left, even though I'm not from there. I figure I look local, but walk American, looking like I know where I am going. Today I'm back in Waldo County with no idea where I am headed, only stuck with where I have and have not been. Nowhere. Anywhere I am is nowhere.

It hurts me to my core to be so much of nothing, to have accomplished so little that now I don't have a home of my own. It's such a cop out to say I've had medical issues, a haunting childhood, or a husband who was not there for me when I needed him most. Lots of people have had any of those things. I put a lot of myself into raising my children, but should have been able to do that and be successful in business, too. I could have if I weren't damaged goods, if there were more to me. I left headed for greatness and have crawled back a sorrowful soul.

I feel like pulling over to cry, but I keep going. That's all I can ever do. I keep going, keep driving. I thought I might be on my way through to the town of Frankfort, but not yet anyway. I keep expecting to come to something I recognize, something to pull me back in a specific direction. I love the woods, the pine needle floor, but now I want something else. I want to go home, even though I don't have one of my own.

I've taken a few turns along these roads today, and now feel more lost than found. I want to get back to the house, to eat, to relax, but I keep going. When I see a sign for Newburgh I realize I've been going north, not east as I thought. I guess at a few turns and recognize a dormered cape, a house I've passed on the road to Bangor. I know where I am. It's not home in Monroe, but now my mind has a way to get me there.

It's early afternoon when I get back to our house and Martha is home. I tell her I don't know where I've been. I say, "I kept going. That's all I can do."

# Planning

Money is the root of all folly. It feels that way for me; I feel a fool. I'm bright enough to be okay and yet, I'm not. Here in Monroe I know I have bottomed out; back in Amesbury I kept planning to do better, sure I could do better. I thought of myself as an optimist as in, "I believe I'll earn my next commission check soon enough." To think otherwise would have been negative and I didn't want negativity in my life. So, I became a believer. I believed it would all work out and now it hasn't, I have to figure out what else to believe. I have to work out a plan.

That's what I do up in my back rooms at Martha's house. I'm in a mess so I plan my way out. Plans start with lists so I list everything I plan to do. I list what is wrong with me, what I plan to do about it. I list goals but remember goals require action plans, so I list all the ways I can get to my goals. I list small tasks, big tasks. I list affirmations; I list my debt. I make my lists on my computer, on graph paper, and in notebooks and journals. Every day I add to my lists and edit what I have so far. I have long-range plans and short-range plans. My lists show this.

*find a job*
*buy the newspaper*
*get gas*
*weed the garden*
*eat healthy*
*rearrange my space*
*write something*
*write a better list*
*do some laundry*
*sew something new*
*find a way to earn a living*
*keep my meds up to date*
*go to Belfast, look for a job*

*go to Bangor, look for a job*
*find a book to read that will solve all my problems*
*check for jobs online*
*call for help*
*go for a drive*
*visit my parents' graves*
*organize my lists*
*work on the first-time homebuyer workshop*
*send in a workshop invoice*
*keep track of my money - what money?*
*figure out what to do next*
*figure out what is wrong with me*

I organize the list, but before I start another one, I do some of the things on this list. First, I choose the things that don't take any cash so I tend to my flower garden, look through my books, and head out for a ride to figure out what is wrong with me. What else can I do? I decide to make a visit to my parents' graves at the top of Knox Ridge. This never cheers me up, but sometimes I do it anyway, hoping it might. It does somehow fill some sense of obligation. I can't be all bad, if I am a person who stops to talk, who tries to keep the connection going. Even if they are dead, they are my parents.

It is ironic two people born as Irish Catholics are now buried in the cemetery for a Baptist Church. Two city dwellers from two different countries, although with one ethnic background, are laid to rest aside Route 220 on top of a windswept ridge. It was years, decades, before I could put flowers on their graves. To do that meant finally acknowledging they were dead. I knew they were, but didn't want to make it any more real than it already was. I didn't want to be a good daughter, I told myself, I wanted to be the daughter of living parents. For many years I was more focused on being a good mother and, I continually told myself, it would not help to look back.

That attitude kept me away from my own childhood. Looking back was travelling backwards and I didn't want to go there again. I was busy singing "Onward Christian Soldiers" under my breath, not for religious reasons, but for the tone of perseverance. Keep on going, marching as to war. Keep on truckin'.

Well, that truck's run out of gas. Now I am back in Maine with barely any ability to look forward, to believe there is a forward for me. Some days I'm stuck, lacking the ability to look outward at all. Those are the days I make lists, using my pen as a shovel to dig my way out, to write my way through it. Today is one of those days.

I hook a right at the top of Knox Ridge and quickly come up to the church driveway on the right opposite the cemetery itself. There is barely any traffic, but I know if something does come it will be speeding by. I cross the road carefully and enter the cemetery by ducking under a heavy chain. After some years of doing this, I realized the chain unhooks, but I still either duck under or step over depending on my mood. Other gravestones here hold local names I recognize. Bryant, Kenney, Peavey.

Once when our kids were little, we stopped here on the way home to Massachusetts from Thanksgiving at Uncle Dan's in Old Town. I was showing my children their grandparents' graves when I noticed I was missing one of my three. I panicked because I couldn't see Luke, who had just turned four. There was snow on the ground, but no other tracks except ours. We had parked the car right next to the cemetery, not across the road. I couldn't believe I came here and lost one of my own children. Here next to my lost mother, I thought I messed up somehow or the universe was being enormously unfair, but we checked the car and, yes, there was Luke in the back seat. We had marshmallows in there and he said he liked them better than the cemetery so he went back to the car to eat them. Loss avoided. I had become a fully engaged mother though I don't know where or how I learned or even if it is something you can learn.

Today I'm looking down at my parents' graves, hers on the left, white marble and slightly upright, looking much older. She has an art deco design reaching between the two dates and her stone reads:

## HELEN F O'LEARY
## 1902          1959

My experience tells me ten years is not enough. I should have been able to have my mother longer. She had, as I recall, or as I recall people telling me, brown eyes. Exotic for us. I apparently look like her except I, along with millions of other Irish, have blue eyes. I always thought I would develop a heart condition, whatever that may be, because she had one, but I got breast cancer instead. I don't know what else she and I do, or do not, have in common. I have always made it up as I go along.

At one point I had decided to be like her but came to admit we can't ever be just like anybody else. Because I only have bits of memory not a whole picture, to me she is an unfinished jigsaw puzzle. The whole is known or was known, but not to me. I had to assemble the pieces and I have never been able to do that without resorting to my imagination to fill the empty, frustrating spaces. I have spent a lot of myself trying to assemble my lost mother.

His stone is on the right, gray granite lying flat:

## DANIEL J O'LEARY
## MAINE
## CSGI      USNR
## JAN 13 1903      DEC 11 1966

He's not such a mystery. I was eighteen when he died of lung cancer. I remember the small thin man who smoked Camel cigarettes and drank instant coffee with evaporated milk. He never missed a newscast and talked politics more than I listened. I don't remember him listening to me. We weren't close. We were both too lonely to even know how to interact and what interaction we had wasn't good.

I wonder how disappointed they would be that their youngest came to be so much of nothing. I try to explain, through an attempted telepathy with the dead or with them anyway, I have produced three awesome grandchildren. I wonder if they would be willing to skip a generation accepting my offspring in lieu of myself. I nearly beg them, in prayer-like fashion, to do so. That's when the dichotomy sets in again. It happens when I try to figure out who I am, whenever I go on that perennial search again. Am I a success or am I a failure?

In the early seventies, one year out of college, I was working as a ballroom dance instructor in Boston after going through a training program at a Fred Astaire Studio. That was interesting in the beginning, but my interest did not hold. I decided if I'm going to remain poor, I might as well do something more remarkable than waltz, cha-cha, and trying to get people to sign up for dance lessons. I answered an ad in the Village Voice for a program called *Sherut La'am* (Service to the Nation). It involved living in Israel for a year including spending a few months in an *ulpan,* a Hebrew school for immigrants. As a result, I am mildly conversant in and can actually read some Hebrew, but I am not fluent. So what is that, success or failure? At the same moment I have been a successful realtor and an abject failure as a businesswoman, a great mother who never did enough, a world traveler who didn't get around much. For my first few summers attending the Women's Writing Retreat, my goal during the year was to be the same person in my everyday life as I was there. I have achieved that now; I am more of who I want to be. Well, I would be, if I didn't feel so miserable.

At the cemetery, I apologize for being nothing and then defend myself. I got a bachelor's degree at a good college four years after I started and have been to Ireland, the Alps, and the Middle East. I lived long enough to raise my children who, by the way, did not grow up in poverty. Stretched finances sometimes, but not poverty. This visit is not working out well, so I pack up my thoughts and leave the cemetery. For whatever reason, once I am back in my car, I decide to head down Knox Ridge to drive around Freedom Village as if that would cheer me up. It doesn't. It occurs to me now, since my childhood home is gone, there will never be a plaque on it saying I once lived there. That was one of my childhood fantasies. *I'll show them, I'll become famous.*

I turn back to Monroe to start another list of things that would help me keep on going. Once at the house I sit still, squeeze my eyes closed, put each hand on either side of my head, daring a headache to come on. Sometimes, right before I start crying, I can come up with an idea by doing this. Today's idea is I need money. I already know that; now I have to figure out how to earn it. So far a list has not helped and a trip to the cemetery got me looking back, not forward. Maybe a book will do it. I take out *The Energy of Money* by Maria Nemeth. She has a PhD which means she persevered through school more than I did. She must know something about success. Her book has a list of 12 Principles for Personal Fulfillment. Great, a list. I can work with that. The book explains to me my relationship with money can be very emotional, draining my energy. The book is right.

I decide to look for a local job. I already have the job as a real estate consultant, but it is nowhere near full-time. Getting paid requires sending in an invoice to a non-profit in Haverhill, Massachusetts, and waiting until they pay me. This is not working out as well as I had hoped. I thought I would send in the invoice and maybe a week or so later, they would send me a check. No. It goes to someone's desk and apparently sits there. In due course it makes its way to accounting where outside vendors such as myself are paid every two weeks. This process can take a month or more. The consulting gig doesn't provide enough income for even my reduced expenses lifestyle, so I also need a steady job, at least part-time, in Maine. When the local paper, *The Republican Journal*, comes out every Thursday, I scour the ads for anything that might be appropriate. Most of them are absurdly inappropriate. Heavy lifting is out of the question, I don't have a commercial driver's license, and it would not be at all cost effective to get to some of these places every day. Belfast, likely the nearest place for a job, is fifteen miles away from Monroe. Most of the jobs are further down the coast. When people advertise for waitstaff, I'm pretty sure they are not looking for an overweight middle-aged woman who tires easily.

I answer an ad for a group home in Belfast and get an interview. On the appointed day, I first drive past the place, going way too far. I arrive only a few minutes late. The residence is sparkling clean, but also sparse. The young woman who interviews me is nice, but none of the residents are there. I don't get to meet them. The job pays less than similar work in Massachusetts, but I'm still interested. I have worked in a house with some men, some women and with all women. This one is all men, young men. I feel tired already. The interview goes well so I leave thinking this might work. A few days later, I am offered a part-time job of two shifts, but the shifts are only two hours each. It's thirty miles round trip to Belfast; I'll be taking home about thirty dollars a week. After paying for gas, I'd be doing little more than breaking even. No cure for depression, not to mention money woes, in this situation. I decide to keep looking.

My daily attire has become the same clothes I wear for gardening. I decide each day which sneakers to wear with the same jeans I wore yesterday. Only my T shirts show variation and even they are boring me lately. Lots of colorful shirts might as well be gray now, but I know I have to keep on going. I have to keep on searching until my colors brighten again. I'm still a believer. I believe it will all work out and although it hasn't yet, I still believe it will. I'm working out a plan to earn more money. I can dig my way out of this, but it won't be today or this week. I have to hope it will be this lifetime.

# Gratitude

Brigid has ended the relationship with her boyfriend which breaks up that household. She is moving to a new place and so then is Luke. Since he can only have one cat now, I am getting back two of the family cats, Buddha and Girlfriend. He is keeping their mother, Victoria. Martha has a dog named Angelica who we always call Jellie. For a dog, she's pretty low maintenance. Out on her run in the morning and in at the end of the day for supper unless it's cold or raining, or, God help her, if there is lightening when she panics and barks. She's a tall, skinny black dog with short hair. She is part greyhound or maybe I think all tall skinny dogs are part greyhound. I'm not a dog person, but she and I get along fine.

Once I come back to Monroe with the two cats, Martha and I head into the winter with three pets in the household. At least that's what I am planning when Matt announces he and his roommate are giving up the house in Kittery. He will be staying with friends in an apartment, going to visit his girlfriend Gretyl who is spending a semester in Galway, Ireland, and will be looking for a new place right after Christmas.

"Will you be able to take Cammie at Martha's for a while?"

He wants to know if I can take care of his cat, another one of Victoria's, from her first litter. Buddha and Girlfriend are from her second. So we head into winter with four pets in the household - a skinny dog who only answers to her nickname Jellie, Buddha the long haired tom cat with the colors of a creamsicle, his sister the multicolored Girlfriend with little splotches of orange color, and Cammie, the sister from another litter with big splotches of color.

I am a person who would be happy with no pets. I could live in the city, alone, but instead I am living with a friend and four animals on forty acres on a dead-end dirt road. Yet when I wake up each morning, I am grateful to be here. It sometimes does not pay to make plans or think you know yourself. This is not what I planned, not what I want, but it's not all bad either.

I am still teaching the first-time homebuyer workshop and have found a part-time job as an insurance inspector. I get emails assigning an address to me, drive out to the subject house, take a picture, and email a form back to the company. For this duty I am paid a pittance that about covers the cost of my gas. I try to make each run a part of another trip; anything south of here I do on the way to or back from Massachusetts.

When I get a request to check out a property in Winter Harbor, I remember my trip to Blue Hill in August. Although this is not on my way to anywhere, I decide to do the job in part because it could be a nice ride that will keep me out of trouble – that trouble being moping around the house in Monroe. I again head out Down East over the Waldo-Hancock Bridge spanning the Penobscot River and drive along Route 1/Route 3 in the general direction of New Brunswick, Canada. If I have been past Ellsworth on Route 1 before, I don't remember it. We did go to Bar Harbor for a high school senior class trip. That would have kept us on Route 3. There was no official class trip so some of us went to Bar Harbor one day instead of school. Quite a wild thing for me to do since, including that day, I was only absent a total of three days in four years of high school.

Today I am barreling along singing to myself and taking in the scenery when I realize the views aren't merely nice, they are incredible. I drive along saying to myself, did I really see that? Did I see something that beautiful? Ocean, woods, hills, and islands – nearly every bit of scenery I could possibly expect comes in and out of view. I try to live with a sense of gratitude and today that sense is welling up in me.

Finding the property is not difficult, I did MapQuest before I came and have the printout with me. I snap a few photos of a nondescript little row house that looks like former military housing and head off to treasure. Because I initially passed my intended location, I'd been all the way to a sign that said ACADIA NATIONAL PARK and I am headed back there laughing at myself. I didn't know the park came this far east. I thought it was only on Mount Desert Island, but that's not where I am. I'm at the tip of the next peninsula over, in a northeast or down east direction. I am at Schoodic Point and apparently on this day have a national park road pretty much all to myself. I drive in, no gate house, no payment, an open entrance. I drive around the twisted road keeping to the posted speed limit. No reason for me to go fast anyway, I'm not going anywhere. Eventually I come to a parking lot where I stop the car, walk around a little, and take some pictures of the expanse of ocean lying before me.

Sitting on one of the huge boulders that line the rocky shore, I start crying at the beauty I am taking in and the gratitude I feel for getting here today. It occurs to me I only have one problem. I don't have enough money. How lucky am I, to have only one problem? My health is good, with issues, but all under control. I have three grown children who love and respect me. Each of them is doing well or well enough. I have no bitter battles brewing, not even with my ex-husband. I have great support from my friends; I have friends who are practically family. I suppose I could be lonely because I don't have a man in my life, but I'm not. Time enough for that. Today I am grateful. Today I feel more alive than I have in a long time.

*    *    *    *    *

Life goes on in a good way leading up to the November 2004 election. Martha and I both support the same candidate, but there is no sense putting a John Kerry sign in front of the house. The only people going by are the ones who live in the few houses past ours and they already know us and how we feel. When I go to bed Tuesday night, there is still some hope Kerry will pull it off. By morning, there is not. Martha and I both remember him from his Vietnam Vets Against the War days around Boston in the early seventies. We are still hoping for peace, but it is not to be. George Bush has won re-election.

A few days later, when I am in the car driving alone to Massachusetts for the workshop, I worry about the people who will die to continue this war, of what those losses must mean to their families, both American and Iraqi. I feel my mood sloping downward.

I'll have to be upbeat to teach the class, but I do not feel good inside. Working like this is like trying to eat something in polite company when there is a bad taste in your month. I won't bring up politics in the workshop, but my immediate problem is not the state of the nation. My problem is the state of my brain. I have again been sucked into a downward spiral and have to work my way out. I had thought after my day at Schoodic Point I wouldn't need to start this all over again. I thought I had cast aside some emotional weight, but now I am again trying to struggle through heavy fog. Trying to search for meaning, looking for healing. I am in the slow process that has no obvious resolution. Getting out of a depression can be like having a fever break, but usually it is not. More often I notice I am a little better now than I was yesterday and maybe even a little better than the day before that.

My previous experience with depression gets me through the worst of this bout until I am back to a bearable baseline. I have to be patient with myself, to expect a process not an event. I wear comfortable clothes, get some favorite foods like potato chips and ice cream, and make sure I do not spend too much time alone.

By Christmas I've done some shopping, getting what I could afford for each kid. Some of it is photos of their cats. Matt took my digital camera to Ireland and gave it back to me with some pictures in it so I enlarge one of him and Gretyl at the Cliffs of Moher and make it a Christmas gift.

I remember going to those cliffs on a family trip to Ireland during Thanksgiving week in 1993. Our first full day in the country, I said we should go see some cliffs and a tower. They each had a look as if to say *okay, whatever.* Driving through an area known as the Burren in November does not yield the scenic greenery and quaint images a tourist might expect. It's more like moonscape. The kids were pretty unimpressed until we got to O'Brien's Tower atop the Cliffs of Moher.

"We didn't know you'd mean cliffs like this, Mom."

"Wow, these are real. They don't even have guard rails."

The Cliffs of Moher stretch for five miles along the west coast of Ireland and range in height from about four hundred to seven hundred feet. O'Brien's Tower, built for tourists in the mid 1800s by one enterprising Cornelius O'Brien, is about halfway up the coast from the cliffs' southernmost point, Hag's Head. I had come to these cliffs alone in the 1970s when I first visited Ireland. I knew my husband and kids would enjoy this site. They didn't quite believe, until they got there, any cliffs and a tower I knew about were going to be as spectacular as they actually were.

This year a trip to Europe is out of the question for me, but not for Martha. She and her sister Alwina are spending Christmas in Rome. Sometimes I'm surprised by what bothers me and what doesn't. I might have thought I'd be enormously jealous, but I'm not. I want to travel again, but not by scraping together some money that I should be using to pay some other responsibility. I remember going into the historic General Post Office in Dublin in 1993 to convert one thousand dollars into the Irish *punt*. It was cash. That's how I want to travel. I'd use a debit card; I wouldn't charge anything. I want to travel again when I have enough money to do it without a strain. Until then I'll hold down the fort here in Monroe.

On Christmas Eve I am alone, waiting for the boys to arrive. Brigid has to work during the day at Whole Foods, and she's going to her dad's for the night. She'll be coming up during the day tomorrow. If I were still living at the lake house in Amesbury, I'd be going over to the party at Carol Maxwell's house. Instead, I, along with one dog and three cats, roam about this place until I finally settle down to watch TV in the evening. I get all the way through Midnight Mass from Rome, taped and aired at midnight here, and still no boys. I have repeatedly told myself of course my two boys are not going to die in a car crash on Christmas Eve while I wait alone for them. Who would even think of such a thing?

The flash of headlights looping onto the circular driveway is a great relief. I go out to greet them as if I were calm. Luke is the first one out of the car.

"Boy, we went on some back roads to get here!"

"Luke, honey, you're on a back road when you're here. There is no other way to get here."

Matt explains, "Well, we made this little mistake. Maybe a big one. We drove past Augusta on the highway, but didn't know it until we saw the signs for Waterville. We got out the big blue book of maps and figured it out page by page. Merry Christmas, Mom."

I have told them when you make a wrong turn around here, you won't go a few blocks but more like a few miles out of your way. They have traveled a lot of extra miles, but they're here.

"Look, Mom, stars!"

Luke still seems impressed he is in the country even though right now he lives in western Massachusetts, near the Vermont border, not exactly city. I'm grateful they are here. We go inside to get warm and have some of the too-much-food I made for a few people to celebrate the holiday. All is well. There is peace on my little portion of the earth tonight. Once I finally get to bed, it is an easy sleep.

The kids have told me I announce every year, Christmas will be okay, maybe not outstandingly awesome, but we'll be fine. I always thought I came up with that new, each year. I had no recollection of saying it the year before, even if they reminded me the year before that I say it every year. I guess I want to soften the blow. They won't get everything they want, but we'll be fine. I have tried to explain to them we can't afford much, but they laugh, chuckle really. The anxiety is mine, not theirs. They know even if I were overflowing with money, getting everything is not the point of Christmas. We always have a good time and this year is no different.

Brigid arrives in time for dinner and still all is well. I have made a new dessert using a recipe I adapted from a cookbook online. The name of it is Peanut Butter Pie and I expect Matt, especially, will like it because he has always liked peanut butter and peanut butter cups. Sometimes things work out. The pie is a huge hit and becomes an instant family favorite after one serving. I sense a new tradition arising. I left out the crushed peanuts (Matt does not like crunchy peanut butter; the others don't care.) I tweaked the amounts and now I have a new favorite recipe that can be made easily.

This basic Christmas could become one of our most memorable. I anticipated a wreck of myself and yet, it all came out to be beautiful. I feared my first Christmas back in Waldo County would bring up all sorts of the less than idyllic memories. I might have focused on being a lonely little kid sorely disappointed each December because my father didn't seem to realize parents buy Christmas presents for kids. I'm not at all disappointed this year. I have three kids and they are all here. We exchange pleasant inexpensive gifts. I get neat body care stuff from Whole Foods, a gardening book, and a Garrison Keillor political satire.

With this Christmas behind me, I'm a little more relaxed but still have to admit I need more of a local job than driving around to check out a house occasionally. I still have my one big problem. I need more money. I have decided 2005 will be the year I disentangle my emotions from my finances. This will be the year I get that problem straightened out. This will be the year I get myself straightened out.

**2005**

*I know there is no straight road*
*No straight road in this world*
*Only a giant labyrinth*
*Of intersecting crossroads.*

"Floating Bridges"
Federico García Lorca

# Treading Water

I love driving in the snow, well some days I do. With a new powder, I don't always clean off the whole car but instead take off down our gravel road with the snow flying off behind me. I am a magic cloud, a burst of white energy. Today I'm on a mission; I'm off to Belfast to buy cat food.

It's February, but I have decided to pretend it is spring because it isn't awfully cold out. Today there is new snow; but it's slush, not the powder I like. Driving in it could require some caution, but I'm an old timer. I've driven in snow before. I get out onto the Oak Hill Road and cross into Swanville, shortly before the Toddy Pond School. The road is slippery, but I feel confident until, in a puff of a moment, I'm crossing the road in midair. Lift off, land. My car sits pointing downward with its front grill kissing a small tree, its rear bumper aligned with the road above.

I decide instantly, this is it. I tried to start over, but no. This is it for me. It ends today. I have crashed my car and my life. Before I can get on to wishing I were dead, two young men appear at the driver's side door.

"Are you alright?"

"You okay?"

"I'm fine."

"We thought sure you were gonna tip over. You crossed the road on two wheels."

They're nice, they're from Maine. They're from across the road. I use their phone to call a tow truck; they even tell me who to call. I'm not injured; I'm deflated. When the tow truck man tells me to get into the vehicle, I hop down from the top of the ditch into deep snow. Feeling myself falling, I put out my hands to brace my body against the body of my car. On my left hand, my little finger bends backward and hurts like hell. Now I'm injured, but I say nothing. I don't want to talk about injuries or stop the process of my car being pulled up onto the road. I want to know how bad my car is. Do I even still have a car?

It comes out of the ditch and is still drivable. It needs some body work, but I continue on to Belfast to get that cat food. I was in a car accident, I think I broke my finger, and I'm grateful. The whole thing is only bad, not horrible.

Weeks go by. I am trying to be happy, but I still have the same old problem. I do not have enough money. The insurance deductible to get my car fixed is five hundred dollars so I am cleaned out. I apply for jobs everywhere, including driving up to Bangor and walking into shops in and around the mall where I ask to fill out job applications. Some places are not hiring; the Borders bookstore only accepts online applications. Some people do hand me a form to fill out, but nobody calls me back. Not the bookstore or even Jo-Ann Fabrics, two places where I hope I have a shot. Nothing. No response from the mall.

Every Thursday I go to the store in Swanville to get the weekly paper, *The Republican Journal*; every Thursday I scour the thing for help wanted ads. One week, I finally spot something that might work for me. The Waldo County District Attorney's office is advertising for a victim/witness advocate. I have never done similar work; but I bet I could, so I send in a resume. I keep looking. I check out online sites as well, and see the RE/MAX office in Bangor is looking for an administrative assistant. I DO NOT want to list and sell real estate again, but finding a job in a field I know may be easier than starting new. I'm beginning to worry about getting a job at my age. I don't think I am too old, but I'm concerned other people will think so. I fill out the online contact form for the RE/MAX job and then start hoping.

I have been contemplating another round of stores or such places, only this time leave out that I went to Bates College, in case I am being disqualified for being overqualified. I could say, truthfully, I graduated from one of the local high schools. I do, after a while, get a call from the district attorney's office to set up an interview. The court job would make that ploy unnecessary. In an interview I could work into the conversation that I am both local and not. I have lived here and *away*, as Mainers call the rest of the world.

My interview is on a Thursday afternoon, but I am teaching the workshop in Massachusetts on Wednesday night. I stay down there on Wednesday, leaving in the morning with plenty of time to get to an early afternoon appointment. On the way back to the Belfast area, I pull into a turnpike rest stop to change into a light green, almost gray blazer newly purchased at the Salvation Army in Salisbury, MA. It's a little too big for me, but I figure at least it's not too small. I complement it with a nearly identical shade mock turtleneck sweater bought in the same store.

I look great, I feel confident, and the interview goes well. The job has set hours, offers little vacation, and does not pay exceptionally well. I make sure to mention that I go away on retreat every July and that doesn't seem to present a big problem. I'm ready. I feel so happy I go right over to where Martha works in the pharmacy at the local hospital, to tell her the news. This could be it. Finally.

I make plans for myself with the new job; working in Belfast is not too far. Eventually I will rent a place of my own there. I won't be able to travel as freely back and forth to Massachusetts to see my kids and I will have to give up teaching the real estate workshop. I can handle all this. My kids are grown. I'm the only one of us going through any separation anxiety over me not having a fluid schedule.

I haven't had any word yet, but I wait as patiently as I can for the phone call or the letter on the Belfast court job. I'm still waiting, but still hopeful, over a week later on a Saturday. I had hoped to get a check in the mail today for teaching the workshop. The past Thursday was the day the agency pays the outside vendors. When I don't get the check on the Saturday, there is a small chance I'll get it on Monday. If not, it is another two-week wait. Right now, it's Saturday night and I am truly bummed because the check did not come and I know that, honestly, Monday is not looking good either.

The evening is off to a bad start. I can only observe things in black and white or shades of gray. I feel there is no color for me tonight when I get a phone call from a woman who owns and manages a real estate office in Bangor.

"Is this a bad time to call?"

Is she kidding? There is no bad time to call me about a job.

"No. This is a good time to call. I'm right here." Of course, I'm right here. It's Saturday night and I'm so depressed I'm lucky I made it as far as the phone.

She sounds nice and, although they have filled the advertised position, she would like to talk to me about working at her office. One of her agents may need an assistant or maybe something else might turn up. She would like to talk to me about the possibilities, and now I want to talk to her. This prospect works for me, tonight anyway. We make an appointment to meet the following week. I'm relieved enough to get through the next few days thinking there is something on the horizon, but I don't want to get excited.

Last fall I did a mailing to all the real estate offices in Belfast and I only heard back from the ones returned undeliverable because the offices had closed. Now I'm still hoping to hear about the job at the courthouse, but I know enough to make the appointment at the real estate office, too. I don't want to sell houses and I don't want to work on commission. I want a job where I show up, do the work, and they pay me. I want the job to be interesting enough to hold my attention, so I'll stay. Other than that, I don't ask for much.

On Tuesday morning I am headed to Bangor to meet people at the real estate office. On the way there, I pretty much convince myself that the manager and her agent, who may need an assistant, are two young go-getters who are going to make me feel even worse about myself and the failure I am. By the time I get to the office, I'm concerned the two of them will snicker, hopefully not until after I've left, about the old lady who showed up for the real estate job. I guess if the whole thing goes badly, I'll go find a bakery and look for something to cheer me up.

I'm wrong. When I meet them, I feel instantly connected and they are much closer to my age than I anticipated. The manager said over the phone her son works in the office, so I don't know how I got the whole age thing going in my mind. We discuss real estate, how it works in Maine, how it works in Massachusetts and New Hampshire (where I also had a license.) The agent has never had an assistant, but she is thinking of getting more into new construction. That's an area where I have experience and it seems like a good fit. We part on good terms. Maybe this will be what finally works for me.

The real estate job is a possibility, but it would be commission based. I want the position at the courthouse. I want the stability, the regular pay. I don't want to have to worry about whether or not I will be paid. I call the courthouse, a few times in a few days. Maybe they are scheduling second interviews, and I want to be included. One day I get the impression the woman who interviewed me won't take my phone call. The next day I get the thanks, but no thanks letter in the mail. Just as well. I have already said yes to the real estate job in Bangor because I was afraid, while trying to juggle two job opportunities, I might end up getting neither.

I start the work in Bangor, glad for the opportunity. Working under slightly different state rules and customs holds my interest. Both ways work fine, reminding me there can be more than one way, but it is interesting to note how the same ends are reached with different procedures. Here it seems the agents get the listing to sell a property, but don't go back to show it. In this office, the showings are scheduled by the woman at the front desk. It all works, but it's not how I'm used to selling. We were always on the phone to our sellers for both scheduling and feedback on showings. This seems more efficient, quite easier for the agent, but less personal for the seller.

I don't have the energy to work in Bangor during the day and sometimes teach a first-time homebuyer workshop on a weeknight in Massachusetts. It's too far. It's physically impossible to do both on the same day so I have to take a day or two off from the real estate office during the week. Now it looks as though the job in

Bangor has more future for me than the workshop, so I decide to quit the whole thing I have going in Massachusetts. Maybe I should rent a place of my own in Bangor. That's what I am thinking, but I'm not happy. Neither job pays enough to live on; one of them is only a portion of someone else's commission.

Life settles into a somewhat respectable pattern. Going to Bangor nearly every day to a job so similar to my old work has me feeling better, but not okay yet. I'm no longer sinking; I'm treading water. I can't quit the job in Massachusetts, I still need the money and I like seeing my friends and family on those trips. When I go there, I sometimes stay with my friend Cathy in Amesbury. Sometimes I head back to Maine but stay with my son Matt in the apartment he has now in Portsmouth, New Hampshire. This helps me feel connected.

We have been offering the workshop one night a week for four weeks in a row. I decide I could do the same thing on two Saturdays, instead of, say, four consecutive Wednesdays – saving me the cost of two trips – the gas, tolls, and coffee to go. The plan gets the go ahead from the manager in Massachusetts and I unquit the workshop job I had decided to quit only days earlier.

It seems I have finally hit a reasonable stride. Work and home are both good. I have enough money for my car payment every month. That's huge – both the payment and the relief I get from paying it. I'm okay. I have nothing going on to excite me, but I'm okay. Maybe this is it. Maybe this is the best I can do.

I'm pleased Brigid is planning to visit, but her trip is unfortunately prompted by her health. We don't know what is wrong. She can't sleep, she can't eat, and she can't settle down. She is exhausted. Her anxiety is overwhelming her and it's having an effect on me, too. We know there is something wrong with her thyroid because she had testing done in western Massachusetts. She's had testing, but no treatment.

Since I have the thyroid condition called Grave's Disease, her symptoms make me wonder if she has it now, too. When talking to my sister Josephine one day, I ask if she remembers Mommy having any thyroid problems.

"Oh, yeah. One day she let me feel a huge lump in her throat."

"Mommy had a lump in her throat?"

"It was huge."

There may be something to this. It could have been an enlarged thyroid, so I call my sister Barbara to see what she recalls. Since both of my sisters are older; they remember our mother better than I do. There is however the complicating factor that they are both adopted. Our medical histories do not align genetically, but maybe they can shed some light on what I might have inherited and passed on.

"Barbara, do you remember Mommy having any thyroid problems?"

"Thyroid? No, she didn't have anything like that. I remember when she had her teeth out, though."

I tell Brigid our medical story will begin with us. Barbara and Jo have a history of remembering things differently, starting with Barbara saying she picked out Josephine in the orphanage. She asked for and got the bald baby. Jo says Barbara does not remember that. I have no opinion on the matter because I wasn't there. I came along years later by accident. Aunt Catherine's version said my two sisters came from the Church. I'm happy to let everyone have their own story.

I'm on the phone with Brigid now but she is in a full-fledged anxiety attack, going on about laundry and a roommate. I know she is not well. It's at least a five-hour drive from here to Bernardston, Massachusetts, near the Vermont border where she moved a few months ago. We have been planning for her to come here, but I wonder.

"Do you want me to come to you or do you want to come here?"

"I'll come there, Mom. I think I can make it."

"Oh, no. That doesn't sound good."

"Don't worry. I want to get in my car and go."

She insists she will be fine; she wants to get away. I know if I drive there, we'll want to leave; but we'll be there with two cars. I want to keep calling her along the road, but I'm afraid I'll tip off the anxiety again when she might be okay, at least briefly. I spend the day worrying until I get a call.

"I'm in Portsmouth at Matt's. I'll see you tomorrow."

She has made it to her brother's place, about halfway. Why didn't I think of that? He gets on the phone, says he has her, and she's okay. Exactly what I want to hear and they know it.

The next day she arrives and seems fine, except she is so thin. I also notice, after a few days, she tires easily. She is on an unpaid medical leave from her job and has canceled all lessons with her figure skating students. She is getting a lot of rest at the house in Monroe, but there is no cure here. Little things like what to eat today set her off; big things like what to do with her life set us both off. I haven't been doing well with my own life this year.

After a few days, we plan to go shopping, one of our favorite pastimes together. She loves it because I pay, and I love that part, too. I'm grateful I can do it again now that I'm working. Bangor is a shopping center for much of northern Maine and nearby parts of Canada. I've heard stories of shoppers coming in from Quebec and the Maritime Provinces with empty or nearly empty suitcases. They remove the price tags from their purchases, take them to a laundromat, and then bring them home as used clothing to avoid the duty fees. During Brigid's visit we are able to take advantage of the full selection of both local and chain stores. Neither one of us has been buying new clothes or much of anything this year, so it's great to finally have an outing like this. It's great to be hanging out with her.

After a few weeks she is more rested, but not any better. We have arguments over stupid stuff. One night I convince her she has to see a doctor, a good doctor who will do more than order tests, someone who will actually treat her. I finally convince her to call Beth Israel Hospital in Boston and she gets an appointment for Thursday of this week.

When she calls her brother Luke to mention it, since he's living in the Boston area now, he points out the timing to her.

"Ah, Brigie. Thursday of this week? That's in two days."

"Oh, I guess I should leave Mom's tomorrow."

"Get to my apartment in Somerville on Wednesday and I'll make sure you get across the city to the hospital on Thursday morning."

This makes me feel a lot better, for two reasons. First, I know she is not sure where she is going in Boston and he can be a big help to her. Her anxiety level is still riding high. When she had her learner's permit, the boys and I had her drive us into the city one Sunday afternoon. My car at the time was a Geo Metro with a standard shift. I didn't want to hear those old refrains from my own daughter, "I can drive, but I don't drive in the city." or "I can drive, but I don't drive a standard shift." We got that out of her system right away. Her 2003 Ford Focus is a standard and she knows roughly where Beth Israel is, but it helps to have her brother go to the appointment with her.

Secondly, in the bigger picture of things, the fact my children are close to each other is one of my greatest joys. As much as I may have messed up my own life, I got motherhood right. I don't feel smug about it. I feel happy for them. It's a relief to know, since I have already had cancer twice, they have each other. I figured out motherhood using common sense, observation of other families, and an effort to provide what I had wanted. I had my moments and we had our trials; but overall, this mother role worked out for me. I'm grateful I have them to love.

As I look around Maine now both my gratitude and my despair expand. The state, as I knew it, has changed. Of course, it has. I had no right to think everything would stay the same while I was off gallivanting. I know you can't stop the tide from coming in. I always thought the core would remain, though. I always thought in a small town you'd never have to lock a door or worry your neighbor's kid would enter your house to get the cash out of your cookie jar or wallet. I was wrong. The people didn't change. Their core remains, but the situation around them has shifted. The way things always were has been altered by drugs. Alcohol is not a new problem, but it was one known to us. This drug use thing is different. It starts much younger, taking away even more of a person's life. We might like to believe such things only happen in the big cities but that is not true. Because the users are so young, they start near home in their local surroundings wherever that may be.

People are doing things they would never have done otherwise, not because of the fatigue from a tedious job or the stress of raising a family on little money. They seem to get started for pleasure; maybe it seems like a cure for teen-aged angst. I don't know, but I feel another wave of gratitude coming on.

From what I do know about such things, I could say I have the predisposing factors for substance abuse. Childhood loss, poverty, emotional neglect in my early years. As an adult I faced illnesses and disappointments overwhelming me, but they did not push me to drink or shoot up or even smoke cigarettes. Sometimes I like a cold beer on a hot summer day, I'll have a glass of wine occasionally, and smoking weed? Well, it never appealed to me much and now with asthma, it doesn't seem like a good idea at all. This is not due to will power. As a matter of fact, if dark chocolate were on the list of abused substances, I would be in no position to be so proud. I have my favorite things; coffee, chocolate, and lemonade to name a few, but they do not make me dangerous to myself or others. For this I am grateful.

# Reunion

I'm working now. Most days I drive the half hour or so to go into the real estate office in Bangor for my job as an assistant. In the beginning, I update a data base of clients and contacts by gathering information listed in various places into a program called RE/MAX Agent. The people in this office seem to think I'm an expert, but I can only be described as familiar with it at best. I did use it myself when I was a RE/MAX agent. Now it is where I keep track of my calendar and the participants for the first-time home-buyer workshop I teach.

I run real estate errands, getting copies of over-sized documents such as a plot plan or picking up paperwork from an attorney's office. I am getting more familiar with Bangor, a city I only knew vaguely when I was growing up in Maine. Now it is a nice place to discover. Every once in a while, I recognize something from a long time ago. One day when going into TJ Maxx, I find myself blurting out, "Zayre's! This was Zayre's." It was the angle of the building that gave it away, a store built into the corner of a strip mall. As it all comes back, I have to laugh. Other days Bangor bears no resemblance to anything I remember.

On the news one night at Martha's house, I heard someone refer to the Bangor waterfront.

"Waterfront?" I asked her. I know Bangor isn't on the ocean. It is on the Penobscot River.

"The river. They call it the Bangor Waterfront now. Lot of people have boats there."

"They cleaned it up?"

I don't remember much about Bangor except it was more working than leisure class. Like a lot of these old places, it had some beautiful large homes from days gone by. In Bangor the wealth was among the timber barons. The surrounding area was heavily forested where now some of these same communities are more like suburbs.

The waterfronts, though, were working areas. I remember seeing the logs floating in the Kennebec River as it flowed through Fairfield and Waterville. These rivers were a way of transportation. I thought it was brilliant that the logs floated downstream to the mills, avoiding any real transport costs as the current carried the load. I was stunned to learn as an adult this whole historic, quaint oh-so-New England custom was a major source of pollution. The logs, the bark especially I believe, killed the river vegetation and therefore the fish and other living things. It was so organic, but it was so wrong. That's how I remember the local rivers, but if Bangor has a lovely waterfront now, all the better.

Working in the Bangor office puts me among some of the nicest people I have met since returning to Maine. The owner is both a good manager and a good person. Her assistant is a hoot. I fit in and feel included. People ask me for my opinion and have questions about how we did things in Massachusetts. I know better than to suggest we did anything any better. As much as I enjoy those discussions and though things seem fine, I'm not happy.

I can't focus on the tasks at hand. The problem is I'm in real estate again. My pay is a portion of someone else's commission. She is generous and honest. There is never an issue of whether I will be paid or not, but my pay is still commission. She is suggesting I get my Maine real estate license. I look into it thinking at the same time - *this is a good idea, this is a bad idea.*

I know if my depression sets in, it will get in the way of earning commission. I feel it. I worry about it and now anxiety is always lurking near the surface. I need this job. I want this job, but I don't want this particular job. I don't want to be a real estate agent again, but what did I think I was going to do? I have nearly twenty years' experience. That qualifies me for a job in, well, real estate. I am getting dangerously close to going back to the commission-only lifestyle that got me up home again wading in poverty.

At one point as we were raising our family, my ex-husband thought it would be a good idea if we moved to Arizona. I was game for a little adventure, but wondered if it was such a good idea for us at the time. When I pointed out to him whatever problems we had in Massachusetts would come with us to Arizona, the idea fizzled since neither of us was committed to it.

Am I doing that now? Am I relocating my problems rather than solving them? Am I bringing my set of issues with me?

One thing is working out better. After Brigid's initial visit at Beth Israel, she was referred to a thyroid specialist who looked at her and said, "You have Grave's Disease. We have to do some blood work to confirm, but I can tell."

Now on medication, Brigid is doing much better. I know from experience this will not be a quick fix, but having a definitive diagnosis is helping her. She is not back at work yet in western Massachusetts, but she got out of the roommate situation there when she and Matt went out with his trailer to get her stuff. She bounces between her brother's places and she stays with me.

I do have one fun event on the horizon, one I never dreamt I would help organize when I graduated from Bates College in 1970. Our thirty-fifth reunion is coming up and I am on the organizing committee for my class. When I was there as a student, I might have been voted least likely to be on the reunion committee, except we probably wouldn't have bothered to vote in a tally like that. If we had, there would have been a lot of competition at the bottom level of interest.

For our fifth-year celebration my friend Janet Freudenberg stayed at my apartment in Cambridge on her way to Maine for the reunion weekend. She asked me why I wasn't going and I remember telling her I hadn't thought of it. I still had some college loans to pay off, and in my mind back then, I wasn't through with school until I paid for it.

Now I have been on the reunion planning committee for years and on a Friday in early June I am driving to Lewiston to spend a weekend, in a dorm room, on the campus of my alma mater. I have a large box of T shirts in the back of my car. I always find myself volunteering to get the T shirts or so-called costume for the Alumni Parade.

Parking is tight in the neighborhood of the college, but I do find a spot on College Street in front of the Quad. The box of T shirts is too heavy for me to carry so I walk over to Roger Williams Hall, which we knew as Roger Bill or The Bill, where my class is staying for the weekend. The campus is being crisscrossed all weekend by golf carts driven by current Bates students known as BatesStars. I don't know if we had any, but I am pretty sure I wouldn't have been one. They help the older alumni get around on campus, but of course I don't need to ride with them. I get to the dorm, greet a few old friends, and realize people are looking for their T shirts so I go out looking for one of the useful students on a golf cart.

I find a nice young lady, give her my keys and say, "Please bring me the box of shirts from the back of my car. It's a dark green Ford Escape parked on College Street in front of the Quad. Maine plates."

She takes off with seeming confidence and all is well until she comes back with the keys, but no box.

"I can't find it," she admits.

I ride with her, retrieve the shirts, and show up again at my class dorm, this time on the golf cart looking, or now at least feeling, like the oldest person in the class.

It's good to see old friends, especially now since we have been out of college for so long. No one calls me out as a failure. No one says: *So, Helen, what have you failed at this year?* Way beyond that nonsense now, we are happy to get together. One of the first people I see is Janet Freudenberg Smith. When we met in 1966, she had a strong south Jersey accent and I had a strong Maine accent. I'd say we meet somewhere in the middle now on that issue.

Larry Delmore is there, too, as always. He is one of the most helpful people on the reunion committee. At one of the planning meetings a few reunions ago, he volunteered to take charge of the entertainment for our class banquet, something I considered a huge job. He leaned over to me and said, "I can't believe you volunteered to do the shirts. I could never do that."

Late morning on the Saturday of reunion weekend, the classes line either side of a walkway leading onto the Quad, youngest classes nearest the finish. The oldest graduates start the parade by walking, or riding in a golf cart, between the lines of the classes ahead of them. Once the last class next to us walks by, we fold into the scheme of things and walk behind our older alumni. We pass a reviewing stand where the costumes are judged by, well I'm not sure who judges them. People who work at the school, I guess. Deans or somebody. We do well to get our class to wear matching T shirts. I can't imagine we would ever be competitive with cool hats and meaningful slogans.

June in Maine is hard to predict in terms of weather. We go through this all the time with the T shirt thing. Some people only want short sleeves; some only want long sleeves. Of course, they do. One year I did an array of choices offering sweatshirts, hats, and the official T for the parade - white polo shirts with the school seal in garnet thread. I got rave reviews for the selection except some women complained theirs was too big. I didn't see that as so bad; it's a lot better than too small.

As we walked in the parade that year, as I was collecting compliments, Larry said to me, "Enough flattery. Keep marching."

An earlier year, before I had anything to do with it, our shirts weren't handed out until after the parade. They were great shirts, a chambray button front, like a lightweight denim, not a T shirt. That was the only year we got any comments from the reviewing stand. We didn't hold a candle to the fifty year class dressed for a toga party or the younger classes with all their graphic arts skills. We caused some confusion and got no admiration as we shouted back that our shirts hadn't arrived yet. I heard much later they had arrived on campus, but the fellow alumni in charge of handing them out got to talking and missed the parade. Our class is not to blame for that one, though. For many years classes were on a schedule that didn't have us meet every five years. Classes would be grouped in threes; that year we were in reunion with the two classes ahead of us. That's when I decided to get involved with the T shirt part of the reunion.

This year I ordered the shirts from a place in Bangor, making sure the shirts would say across the front: *The Past Keeps Getting Better All the Time*. That's our class motto this reunion; we are infinitely clever. Below our motto there is an embroidered bobcat with **Bates College Sesquicentennial** on one side and **Class of '70 35th Reunion** on its other. I joke with the guys at the T shirt place that sesquicentennial must be spelled correctly; there are people who will notice. I don't make a big deal out of it there as we laugh. I know I am one of those people. Our embroidered bobcat is one I picked out of a book of designs when I ordered the shirts. It's cute even if it is not the official bobcat mascot of the college. For all I know it is an embroidered baby lion, but I know it will work fine for us.

Today we have on our heather gray T's, they are long sleeved, and it is at least one hundred degrees out. I am hearing a lot of *why didn't we get short sleeves?* But I know why. Back in January when we asked, the preference was overwhelming for long sleeves. That's why. One woman is looking for scissors to cut off her sleeves before the parade begins.

I don't remember the parade having music in other years, but this year we are led off by a group well known in Maine - The Blue Hill Brass. Four men, four horns and great music. The older alumni pass by us then we join in behind them, getting a few questions at the reviewing stand. "What do those shirts say?"

I keep marching. I am home among friends and glad to be here. I am at a reunion that is a retreat from my normal anxiety.

# More Changes

The real estate job has ended, not with a bang but a whimper - or at least with a quiet agreement we could each do better. My heart was not in the work there, although the experience was a terrific one socially. I loved the people I met in Bangor, some of the nicest people ever, but in spite of that or maybe because of it, I don't belong. I don't want to be a real estate agent and I don't want to work on commission, in the lifestyle that keeps me on the edge of the downward spiral.

I have to do better for myself. I'm not an inherent failure. I can get a job; I'll get another one. I'm searching for something more meaningful, though. I'm searching for something more on the order of Buddhist right livelihood, a call to earn a living in such a way that does no harm towards yourself or others. Selling houses doesn't hurt people. I have enjoyed helping families and individuals find new homes and have self-respect for the fact that my clients considered me a legitimate entity. I sometimes felt more respected by them and my peers than by myself. One real estate agent who knew me well back in Massachusetts had described me by saying, "She won't set the world on fire, but she won't be your next lawsuit either." I'd say that was about right. I wasn't aggressive enough, but I wasn't a legal or ethical problem. I did my job well, but did not round up enough business to keep going.

Although selling houses doesn't hurt anyone else, it wasn't good for me. I was the one I was hurting. I lived over-stretched with stress. I have to do better; I have to take better care of myself. My working life has not yet caught up with my thinking life, but that is my goal. I want a job requiring me to think a lot and paying me on a regular basis.

At the end of July I'm on my way to the Women's Writing Retreat. Once again, I'm taking off on vacation despite barely working. Before my trip I answered a help-wanted ad in *The Republican*

*Journal,* thinking *this job has my name on it.* It doesn't seem to have much to do with right livelihood, but I don't see it would do any harm either. The Chamber of Commerce in Belfast is looking for a director. I'm not sure from the ad exactly what that would entail, but the job is in Belfast and sounds like it could be a good experience both professionally and socially. I could expect to meet other business people I would like. Also, it apparently pays for the time worked with no commission involved. I send in my resume, mentioning I will be away for a little over a week, and take off to the Adirondacks.

This year Margaret took the bus to Bangor and spent last night at the house in Monroe. Today we are heading across Maine, New Hampshire and Vermont towards Lake Champlain where we will cross into New York. I figured this route would be hilly, going through the White Mountains, but what an understatement. There is a reason they are called mountains not hills. We go up and down, up and down, all the while taking in gorgeous views. My cell phone coverage is spotty, but at one point it does ring. Martha is calling from Monroe to say someone from the Chamber of Commerce has called and wants me to call back tomorrow. I knew it. This job is for me.

The trip across northern New England takes us eight hours, but eventually Margaret and I settle in at the Pyramid Life Center where my cell phone does not work at all, not even close. What's a retreat if you are on the internet and cell phone all week? I want to return the phone call about the job so, the next day I leave the site to drive back into Ticonderoga where I do get some coverage. The connection is not good, but the woman I am speaking to, from the Chamber of Commerce, wants to know if I can come in for an interview this week. I want to ask if she read the cover letter I sent with my resume saying I would be away, but instead I say I am in upstate New York and will not be back for almost ten days. We make an appointment for the week following my return and I head back to the retreat center. Margaret, who has come along for the ride into town, suggests we could leave the retreat early so I could go to the interview. I won't hear of it. No way. The retreat has been a constant in my life when I have needed that. The last night is the big one and I'm not going to miss it. I plan to have both the retreat and the job.

I have another great week with women writers at Pyramid Lake. We write, we read, we swim, and we commune. All too soon, the week is over and, after a few days in Massachusetts, I am home in Monroe.

It's quickly interview time for me again. I want the job at the Chamber, but have no idea if I am the one they are interviewing or if I am one of many. Well, probably not many, but I may be one of a few. On the day of the appointment, a gorgeous day in early August, I easily find the yellow clapboard building near the bottom of Main Street. I go inside and up the steps, more steps than seems usual, but it is an old building. Entering the one-room Chamber of Commerce office, I hold back laughter. It is only one room, but it's a big room. There are a few tables arranged in a U shape, and in the middle, all by itself, is the chair for the candidate to be interviewed. I didn't expect this arrangement, but instantly I'm reminded of a Monty Python comedy sketch in which characters, in red robes, dressed like Roman Catholic cardinals shout, "Nobody expects the Spanish Inquisition."

I take my place on the hot seat and we begin. I'm being questioned by four members of the Board of Directors. Two or three of them are real estate agents, so I may have some "in" there. I explain I grew up in the area, but realize all four of the people interviewing me are from away. I'm not sure they actually know where Freedom Village is. The job is for the Belfast Area Chamber of Commerce, but I quickly learn by *Area* they mean mainly along the coast. That's where most of the money is and most of the new people are.

I end up telling them one day in Belfast when I was a kid, my Irish father told me, "You know we have a city by this name at home, too, don't you? It's in the North."

At least one of them finds this interesting. The interview proceeds with polite chatter. It is a part-time job with a commitment for some set hours along with the occasional evening meetings such as the Chamber After Hours Socials and other events. No one else works in the office except a bookkeeper who comes in on Wednesdays. All of the members of the board have other jobs, but attend a meeting here at the office about once a month, usually on a Thursday.

The questions aren't taxing and for my part, the interview goes well. I could easily do this job and keep the workshop in Massachusetts. Between the two, I would make enough money to be okay and Belfast is much closer to Monroe than Bangor is. Things are looking up. The Board of Directors will meet again next Thursday and will let me know soon of their decision.

The following Friday morning, I get the call and I get the job. It pays about one third of the hourly rate of the real estate workshop, but it is local. It's the start of a plan. I will do this along with the workshop and at some point get my own place in or at least closer to Belfast. I feel good.

I can't however start the job right away; I delay a week because Brigid is having surgery to remove a branchial cleft cyst on the right side of her neck. Earlier in the year while she was living in western Massachusetts, she had the same cyst drained. The thing is back, but now she is a patient at Beth Israel in Boston where the cyst will be surgically removed. She has another figure skating friend, also a redhead, who had the same thing. It is a congenital fluke, but one with the potential for infection. She does not need a fluid-filled sac on her neck and will be better off without it.

We spend the night before the surgery at Luke's apartment; and by we, I mean me, Brigid, and her new dog Wookie. Some friend of a friend had a Lhasa Apso that turned out to be too much for their family, so she has gladly taken it on as her new project. She left the puppy with Luke when she went again to the writer's retreat in July. He thought it would be fine to have a little dog for a week, but oh my goodness, a puppy, and apparently a Lhasa Apso puppy, even more so, has a lot of energy and requires much of the 'same from its keeper. Being at Luke's now with Wookie helps me acknowledge that someone could feel this dog is too much. I would.

Although Brigid's surgery goes well initially, she spends the first night at Luke's repeatedly losing the contents of her stomach, to put it nicely. By morning she is drained out. We head back to the hospital where, after a day on IV fluids in the emergency room, she is admitted. After two nights there, she is markedly better. Now we are ready to return to Maine.

I'll be starting my new job and, after getting some rest here in Monroe, she will be moving into a new apartment in Greenfield, Massachusetts, near one of the rinks where she has been coaching. It's nearly autumn again and I'm still here. I haven't fallen off the face of the earth, off a cliff by the sea, or into a personal abyss. I'm still moving along at my own uneven pace, ready once more to start over again.

# Belfast in a Chamber

It is once again the first day of a new job and already I feel fatigued by the thought of it. I wish I were more settled, I wish I were not starting over again; but I am. One more time I'm at the outset of a new phase. I can at least look forward to meeting people, something I usually like. I expect to do that on this job. One of the reasons I want to work in Belfast is to establish myself here with friends, colleagues, acquaintances. Whoever comes along. Today, however, I wonder if that is enough. Today I'm new again but it saddens me. I know new beginnings are my only hope right now since I don't have full-time employment, but what I want is consistency. I'd love to be able to say *things are going great, wouldn't change a thing.*

Brigid is still in Monroe recovering from her surgery. As I leave for work, she gives me a postcard from The Green Store in Belfast. Besides the picture of what looks to me like the Great Wall of China, there is a quote from The Buddha. "There is no way to happiness, happiness is the way." It's a nice gesture from her and I have it with me as I head out.

The Belfast Area Chamber of Commerce is at the bottom of Main Street, on the left before you'd cross over Front Street to get to the municipal pier. Driving down the hill I pass The Fertile Mind, a favorite little independent bookstore; Coburn Shoes, the nation's oldest shoe store according to their sign; and the Green Store, an ecologically correct emporium full of goods ranging from organic cotton clothes to composting toilets. I love this little city. Picturesque but vastly different from the way I remember it, it's great to be working here now. I'm looking forward to this job that seems to be full of what I want. I wish I could shake off the "oh no, starting over again" feeling that is holding me back.

The job at the Chamber is nebulous to say the least. My official job title is Associate Executive Director, but I wonder why they hired someone. One member of the Board consistently refers to me as the Assistant Executive Director although there is no one to assist. There is no Executive Director. I'm it, except for the bookkeeper who comes in on Wednesdays. We don't work on the same day because we share the computer. My official time to be in the office is Tuesday mornings and Thursday afternoons. I work more than that, particularly if there is something in the evening, but not much. I thought the Chamber of Commerce would be a busy place. I thought there would be people coming and going. I know there aren't many people working here, but I had no idea I'd be alone almost all the time. I'm supposed to handle inquiries although anyone who calls from the website, presumably a tourist, will reach an answering service, not me. I'm there to take questions about membership, if there are any. I'm supposed to familiarize myself with the job though I'm not sure what the job is. This leaves me feeling I'm not needed here.

There is an outgoing President of the Board, a pleasant woman who tries to be helpful, and an incoming President who seems a bit overwhelmed, but who also is pleasant. At first they are the only two I deal with, but I learn I do have one particular job, and I'm glad to hear it. It seems to be up to me to do the monthly newsletter. At least I think it is up to me. Each member of the Board of Directors is assigned to a committee or task.

In my first contact with the one who is attached to the newsletter, I'm taken back.

She calls me at the office and sounds terribly put out with me. I have never met her or even spoken to her on the phone before. When I ask her a question, she says something about all this hocus pocus. I have no idea what is wrong. I'm not in a defensive mood today and though the conversation is immediately strained, but I put up with her because I want to do well. Fortunately, at that particular moment, the current President of the Board is also in the office. She is surprised to learn this is my first conversation with the newsletter lady. Even though she only hears the one side, she gets the tone of it. I acknowledge my surprise at the other director's manner, but say I'm sure it will work out.

The Chamber of Commerce has a few committees and all of the members of each committee are Board members. No one except Board members are on any committee. Over the years of my real estate career I've been involved with, or attended functions at least, with the Chamber of Commerce in Newburyport and its counterpart in Amesbury, Massachusetts. Committees had lots of different people on them. When I ask about the arrangement here, I'm told, "We've asked. No one wants to help."

That is one way to look at it, but I can't help wondering why that's the way things are. I wonder why all the committees are just rearrangements of the Board members. Belfast is a city of about six thousand people. Besides the Chamber, it has an uptown business group and a downtown business group. One store downtown also has a store in Brunswick where they do belong to the Chamber of Commerce. Here they do not.

The Chamber ran a summer promotion to decorate the downtown and to raise money. People in the community built birdhouses, ranging from relatively simple all the way to quite elaborate. With the summer over, today is the day the birdhouses are coming down in preparation for Saturday when they will be auctioned off as a fundraiser. The Board members of the Birdhouse Committee are assembling outside the Chamber office. The building also holds a copy center, a camera store, and the Chamber's Visitor Center, staffed by individuals who volunteer. It seems to be nearly autonomous from the Chamber office, except there is a committee for it. It is open only seasonally and it is closed now in the fall. I greet the Board members I see as I go out to pick up some lunch, about three or four of them. A pleasant greeting, nothing wrong.

When I get back, I head towards a parking space a few down from where I was parked before. The cars of the Board members I saw on my way out are still there, and now there is one additional Director parked next to where I am pulling in. She is leaning on her car, eating a take-out sandwich.

"Are you going to be here for a while?" she asks.

"Yes, I'm scheduled to be here for the afternoon."

She points to my car and says, "You'll have to move your car closer to mine. We have to leave room for the businesses in the building."

She seems exasperated with me, that she has to explain something so simple. There are still a few spaces left and there would be even more if there weren't so many Board members parked here today. I back up my car then pull forward closer to hers.

"Will that do?"

"Well, it's better."

As I head into the building, climbing the steep stairs to the office, I think *that was interesting and had little to do with where I was parked.*

When I tell my son Matt about it a few days later, he tells me he would have pulled so close she wouldn't be able to get back into her car. Although that's an interesting idea, it would not be a wise move between two grown women in a professional situation. It's too bad it happened. I'd like to forget about it, but it sits in my mind as a cautionary tale.

Brigid has been feeling better and is back living and coaching in Greenfield, Massachusetts. She was able to find an apartment by calling one of the figure skating mothers who had kept in touch with her when she was sick. Brigid had been worried about the logistics of being able to find a place there by calling around while she was still in Monroe. I said she should try through the people she already knew. She explained to me they are all about ten years old or younger and she only knows them because they skate. I told her I meant for her to call some of the parents starting with the nice lady who had called a few times over the summer.

Brigid called her asking, "Do you know of any apartments available in Greenfield?"

"This might sound funny. I don't know how you feel about it, but we will have our downstairs apartment available soon. Would you be interested?"

Sometimes things aren't difficult. Sometimes things fall into place and I'm glad to see that happen for Brigid. Something else good is happening for her. My friend Cathy is going to Hawaii along with her family. Each of her two children had been planning to go, along with their current boyfriend or girlfriend, but after Cathy's daughter Colleen broke up with her boyfriend, they invited Brigid instead. Brigid is going to Hawaii. This is great for Brigie, but it means I get to babysit the Lhasa Apso.

Wookie is still an energetic puppy. I have her crate, but getting her into it each night is too difficult for me. Maybe a falconer's glove would help, but I don't have one. The dog is both adorable and, while not evil, strong willed at least. Whenever she plays with Martha's dog Jellie, I get nervous. I can't tell the difference between playing and fighting. I'm always afraid one of them will hurt the other. I'm mostly afraid Wookie, the smaller of the two, will hurt Jellie, the most mellow of dogs.

After a few days I lighten up and don't put Wookie in the crate at night. She jumps up onto my bed and sleeps easily. Buddha and Girlfriend, the cats, are not thrilled, but they manage. Wookie loves to ride in the car; she loves to be in the car even when it is not moving. When I go to work at the Chamber, I take her with me. I get her a small-dog-sized rawhide at the store in Swanville on the way into Belfast, and leave the back seats of my car down. This gives her much more room than any crate would. She doesn't chew up the car; she usually waits on the driver's seat for me to come back. I can see her sleeping there from the window of the chamber office and fortunately she does not bark at people who walk by the car. We have found our rhythm. I wish I could say the same for my job at the Chamber.

# Holidays Again

The holiday season starts off in mid-November with Wookie's first birthday while Brigid is in Hawaii. Since I promised Brigid we would celebrate, Martha, her granddaughter Mya, and I don Winnie the Pooh party hats, taking pictures to document the event. The kitchen in Monroe becomes party central with Martha and I laughing at ourselves. Mya, now three years old, enjoys the dog birthday party; Wookie doesn't seem to care much either way. Both dogs get treats, we eat orange frosted cupcakes bought in the supermarket, and we wash it all down with ginger ale. Let the holidays begin.

Another pre-holiday occasion is the Chamber of Commerce Annual Meeting and Dinner on the Saturday before Thanksgiving. A few weeks before the event, I am told to update the invitation for the Chamber dinner, using last year's as a model. Each invitation will be one sheet of autumn themed paper much like a flyer. I include the new information, change the layout and fonts a bit, then leave it out in the office for the current president to see. She is going to drop in; I am heading out to lunch. When I get back, she has come and gone leaving me a note saying to please make this year's invitation more like last year's. Well that's creative, I think, and change the whole thing back. I don't know why it has to be a copy of last year's invitation, but we are, at least, using different background paper this year and changing the date.

At a planning meeting comprised of me, the current president, and a former president, we go over the menu. I hear, "We will have this, this, and this, but not this. No green beans, absolutely no green beans. These people don't do green beans right."

*These people* are a local catering company who does a nice job, but they are not members of the Chamber. I suggest we have some of our member restaurants do different parts of the dinner to showcase their specialties. *If looks could kill.* We go with the local catering company.

On the morning of the dinner a few of us are at the site to set up tables and decorate them. We have balloons and centerpieces, much like last year's. By this point, I'm trying hard to do what I am told. This is not easy for me, because it isn't in my nature and because I wasn't at last year's dinner. It seems everything I do or suggest is wrong.

Tonight's event is also the annual meeting. The new officers will be sworn in and there will be a vote on the roster of upcoming board members. Even if everyone who RSVP'd to the invitation attends tonight's dinner, there will not be a quorum. I am sent out among the downtown retailers, most of whom will not be attending tonight, to rustle up some more votes. I want to ask, "Now what exactly did the person who did this last year say?", but I don't. I head out, glad to be on my own. A few people sign the ballot, I think to get rid of me, and one because I think he feels sorry for me. He teases he won't sign it, even as he is doing so. One woman says she doesn't know any of these people so she doesn't feel she should vote. I don't blame her. I've heard some discussion among a few members of the Board of Directors that a quorum may not even be necessary. I'm still trying to do what I am told.

Before I go back to Monroe for what is left of the day, I have to stop into the local Rite-Aid to buy panty hose. I'm pretty sure I don't have any and the evening is dress up. This puts me over the top. I buy the panty hose, but find myself resenting the purchase. It can't be the dollar amount, they aren't that much. It's buying anything for this job. If I wanted a job that costs money, I could have stayed in real estate.

After I shower and start to get dressed for the big night out, my mind muddles. What I had planned to wear, a sleek silver skirt, looks all wrong. It's too tight, too dressy, not dressy enough, just wrong. I settle on the black velvet skirt I wore to my Aunt Catherine's funeral and top it off with a nice, soft, red sweater. I don't like my shoes, black slip-ons with a wedge heel. They are not too tight, not too dressy; they are not dressy enough. Who, though, will be looking at my feet? By early evening I have no choice, though I don't want to go. Some of my real estate friends from Bangor are at a holistic weekend workshop; I'd prefer to be with them. The topic, Reiki massage, is a bit touchy-feely for me, but right now it sounds better than touchy.

I have to be at the dinner, although I briefly entertain the idea of calling someone to say my daughter is sick or I'm sick or my car hit a deer or I forgot. I stop procrastinating and trying to distract myself and finally make the drive into Belfast. My head is still trying out lame excuses when I arrive to work the table at the entrance to the dining area, checking people off to see if they have paid, and to give them their name tags. I put my purse and an extra tablecloth, not needed after all, on the floor behind me. One member of the Board comes over to tell me to move those things because members of the press will be taking photos of the speakers and my things will show up. She motions with a long arm to show me precisely where the press will be aiming. This is the same woman who asked me to move my car. If she had a pistol, would she shoot at my feet to see me dance? I'm sure any local reporters who take pictures will not be including the floor in their shots, but I move my things anyway.

Before the actual dinner begins the attendees mill about, drinks in hand. There is a silent auction, with some nice items donated from Chamber members, including a large bowl with their pine tree design from Monroe Salt Works, a lobster utensil kit for help in eating the pesky but much-loved local fare, and some handmade Irish pottery from the local import store Shamrock, Thistle, and Rose which is co-owned by the outgoing Board president.

After the initial socializing, the attendees take their places at round tables seating about six to eight people. The members of the Board for the most part clamor for tables right in front of the podium. There is no attention paid to the fact that a few of those seats are meant to be reserved for the guest of honor representing MBNA, the Company of the Year. I don't see anywhere to sit at first, but find a seat with people from Renys, a Maine retailer with a store in the uptown shopping area of Belfast. I introduce myself as the Associate Executive Director, explaining it is a new position. They are not impressed and frankly, neither am I by this point.

The outgoing president emcees the evening, introducing each of the Board members and the recipient of the Company of the Year award, thanking all of them for their commitment to the community. She talks about her year at the helm, including changes that have occurred during her term of office, but makes no mention of the new position I hold. I must be invisible. The speeches, the introductions, the presentations go on and on, but there is some good news. In the silent auction I have the winning bid for the handmade pottery from Ireland. There will be something nice for me as a takeaway of the evening.

Immediately after hosting the ceremonies, the now former president comes directly over to me to apologize. "I didn't think to mention you, even though you're new. I probably should have said something."

Well yes, she should have. It would seem normal to mention a new position at the Chamber, no matter how anyone may feel about me personally. I can't help but laugh to myself. The speaking has finished only seconds ago. She could have thrown in mention of this new job at the end. I wonder if the people at my table think I am lying when I say I am the Associate Executive Director. Probably not, but they do get to see how unimportant the title is.

During a brief break down session immediately after the dinner, I try to be friendly but it is difficult. I am here among people who have looked at me askance since I started the job. Their dislike of me only feeds a similar feeling from me towards them. I'd say we are in a loop. You know when you are among people who are not your people. It is awkward, but they seem to be trying, too. I am offered a drink, but don't want one. I don't drink much and right now, I prefer to get on with it and go home with my two new matching auburn and creamed-corn yellow pitchers from Ireland. The party is over and we all made it through.

In a few days, just before Thanksgiving, I am driving to Luke's apartment near Boston. This should take me at least four hours, probably longer, so I settle into one of my deep thought modes.

Crossing the new bridge in Augusta, high over the Kennebec River, I look upstream towards Waterville into a misty view and get a little bit misty myself. Leaving the state of Maine for a holiday instead of coming into it is different for me. Going to my son's house for a holiday dinner seems new, as if a generation has passed. I like the feeling. It seems like a gentle progression in time. It feels as though things are moving along nicely.

Thanksgiving Day itself is engaging. I may be a guest, but I am also the mother, which means I am cooking the turkey. We all work on the meal and it becomes a lot of fun jostling for space, giving each other advice. Luke's girlfriend is spending the holiday with her family, so she's not around though she lives here, too. Matt has come down from Portsmouth and Brigid has come in from Greenfield in western Mass. My ex-husband and his wife come for dinner and it is a nice family event.

Sometimes people are amazed we would all spend a holiday, or any day together. Resentment toward my ex-husband might make more sense. Even my aunt expressed surprise a few years ago when I told her he and his wife had come over to my house at the lake for breakfast on Christmas morning. I'm sure he should have been there for me when I got cancer after twenty years of marriage and three children together. I *do think* he should have stuck it out. I *don't think* carrying around resentment or acting on it would be helpful for anyone involved. I know it would not be good for my mental health.

Once Christmas arrives this year, I'm off again for another family adventure in Massachusetts. The boys and I are going to be at Brigid's apartment in Greenfield where she has enough room for the three of us to visit. She has decorated her place for the holiday and even set up a tree by herself. A few weeks earlier she spotted a sign that read CHRISTMAS TREES 10 DOLLARS. She pulled in, planning to pick out her tree and drive home with it sticking out of the trunk of her car. At the end of a long driveway a man handed her a saw and pointed her toward the trees. She did get his help getting her selection into her car, but she had cut the tree down herself. As Luke said, "We have to go to Brigie's this year. She chopped down her own tree."

I arrive at Brigid's on the 23rd and present her with a new coffee maker. When she asks if it is an early Christmas present, I explain she can think of it that way if she likes, but really I wanted to make sure I got coffee in the morning. We go shopping together for all the food for the holiday and I'm glad I have the money to get everything we need. The Chamber job is not what I had hoped, but it does take the edge off the financial problems I face.

On the day of Christmas Eve, Brigie and I make whoopie pies, a real Maine treat. They are much more than two chocolate cookies with a white cream in the middle. That's what they look like, but the recipe calls for vinegar, Crisco, and sugar. It is a special taste, but not one you would call an acquired taste; they are usually an instant hit. They are also fattening so I only make them at holidays or birthdays. Brigid and I have fun baking together. I'm grateful for the time with her.

In the evening we are waiting for the boys to show up. Matt is driving down to Cambridge to pick up his brother and they will head out to western Mass. together. Luke is working at a Whole Foods in Cambridge and has had to work on the 24th. Like last year, the car becomes their own parallel universe and once again they drive too far. They do arrive, though later than we planned. I am so happy we are all together again. Once they are at Brigie's we eat whoopie pies and each of us opens one gift, one of our old Christmas traditions. Again, all is well in my world.

In the morning as we unwrap gifts, I am reminded I like the way we celebrate. The gifts are modest, but individually appropriate, or so I think. I got each boy a chamois shirt, blue for Luke and grey for Matt. They look at them, switch them, and we move on.

After Christmas, I return to the Chamber job and back into the gnawing feeling that this is not working. It's a bunch of little frustrations eating at me, but so far no real blowouts. Every month, I work on the newsletter. Every month I put in a request for mailing labels from the bookkeeper. She only works on Wednesdays, so if I make the request on a Thursday, I will not get the printed sheets of labels until I come into work the following Thursday. The funny thing, though, is this is all done on the same computer. I don't have access to the membership list because it is password protected in QuickBooks. It seems absurd to me, but I don't suggest a change because I don't want access to the bookkeeping or the money. The situation is strained enough without getting any money issues thrown into the mix. I go along with the way it is for now, except I do suggest we have a membership database - a stand-alone system. I am told we have Quick-Books and don't need a database.

I thought this job would be right up my alley, that I would meet new people in the area and it would be a way to make a new home for myself in my old surroundings. But no. For the next Board meeting I have everything set up when one of the directors arrives, the same one who asked me to move my car and to move my things at the dinner. She tells me to change it all back before the other people come. The tables have to be put back in a U shape. I move tables and food and chairs, but I have to step outside onto a nearby deck in order to cool off - not from any exertion of moving things, but to release the pressure building inside me.

Part of my job is to attend a monthly regional meeting of Chambers of the Mid-Coast area where I am met with some suspicion because I represent Belfast. After I have attended a few of these someone says to me, "Oh, are you going to keep coming?"

"Yes, I was planning on it."

"Oh, we've never had anyone from Belfast attend on a regular basis. We've had a few different people, but no one who stuck with us."

I'm not sure what that comment is about, but coming out of the meeting at The Lighthouse Museum in Rockland, Maine, I see I have a flat tire. Besides the annoyance of it all, I am upset because I planned to go right from this to a Chamber After Hours Social in Belfast. Now I'm going to be late. Fortunately, I am signed up for roadside assistance through AARP. Getting the spare put on tonight is worth the annual membership fee. Once I get to the meeting in Belfast, though, I feel as deflated as my tire had been.

Why did I even bother? There are two women on the Board, the newsletter lady and the one who asks me to move everything, off in one corner, talking with their hands up at their mouths, looking at me, talking some more. Oh, please. I am tired and this is getting tiring. Teenagers are more mature.

Unfortunately, I need the job. There must be some way to make this work, to keep on trucking through this as well. I've been through worse and since this is just a job, we should be able to settle into a working rhythm eventually.

**2006**

*All the untidy activity*
*continues, awful but cheerful.*

"The Bight"
Elizabeth Bishop

# Home Again

There are problems at the job, true, but there are problems developing at the house, too. Martha's daughter, her boyfriend and the granddaughter are all moving in. There is room for everyone, but this is more people than I can take. Martha and I have usually had little Mya on evenings and weekends when her mother worked. I've liked being involved in the little girl's life. She calls me Mama Helen, and we have our fun together, but she eventually goes home.

I want my own place again and things seem to be lining up for that to happen. It's time. Because I have the Chamber job, I'm in a slightly better financial position. I can meet my obligations and feel like a self-sustaining adult once more. I look for a new home for myself, one I can rent despite my financial restraints. I don't need a place big enough for my kids too, but I do take into consideration that I have two cats when I answer an ad for a house on Route 3 in Searsmont. It's a little old house that has been in the same family for a long time. The woman showing it to me says, "I was born in this room," pointing into a small first floor bedroom. The house is okay. I can afford it, but it doesn't do anything for me. It's on a busy corner of a busy road and I am concerned about the cats who have been living near the end of a gravel road surrounded by acreage, not traffic.

I'm still considering the first house when I call about another one in Morrill. I like the woman I meet to see this house and tell her I looked at the one in Searsmont. When I mention that first house was once hit when a car missed the turn, she said, "I know that house. That didn't happen once. It happened twice."

Okay, that news is a bit off-putting, to say the least. She shows me the house she has for rent. It's only $650 a month and it's a cute enough two-bedroom home. She mentions that behind the back yard of this house, she has three trailers she rents, and one of them is available now for $450 a month. She hasn't advertised it yet, but she could show it to me.

We step into the trailer and when I look to the right, I see a bright sunny kitchen. I'm sold. In my real estate career I learned to say mobile home, not trailer, but who am I kidding? I have no need for even a hint of pretension left. I'm going to be living in a trailer, but it is off the beaten path on a sort of cul-de-sac of three trailers and I like the idea. I think Buddha and Girlfriend will like it too. It's a good place for cats to be able to roam without being in traffic.

I'm pleased with myself and my new spending style. I'm more conservative now. I would prefer the house, but I take the trailer because of the price difference. I feel I can live here until my car is paid off, about a year and a half from now, and then I will get a nicer place.

My new tenancy starts February 1st, 2006, and I have every reason to believe this will be a busy month. Bit by bit I move my stuff in my Ford Escape; once again I am living my life with my back seats down and my car full of personal belongings. The trailer comes with a bed, a sofa, and a lot of built-in shelving and cabinets. I have given away my kitchen table and chairs to Brigid, but my friend Carol has a set left in one of her listings. She has to get rid of them and I am the perfect candidate to take them. I liked the ones I gave away - high back chairs in black metal; these are wooden and look like chairs everybody has at one time or another. They are not what I would pick out, but I'm in no position to be picking out anything. I'm grateful at this point for the free table set.

I feel strange inside the trailer at first. My cell phone doesn't work here, I have no land line, no internet access yet. My TV reception is scant. My radio works, so I guess I will know if there is some major crisis such as another 9/11 or a weather emergency. My kids can't call me and I can't reach them so I'm still sleeping at Martha's until I get more of my stuff moved and set up.

I am teaching the workshop two Saturdays this month and working at the Chamber of Commerce a few days during the week. My work keeps me busy, but not so much I can't devote time to the move. The weather is cold and I am paying for my own heat. I keep the thermostat down, but I'm not freezing. I can always put on a sweater. How many times did I tell my kids to do that? How many sweaters do I own? Too many, despite having downsized my possessions so much.

It's fun unpacking the things that have been boxed for almost two years now. I don't like to cook, but I like to have a fully equipped kitchen. It is the most important room in a house to me even though cooking itself is not at the forefront of my mind. It's still the room with the pulse. Unpacking what I saved from my own pots, pans, and kitchen gadgets is a reminder of my previous life at the lake house. I gave away most of my dishes, but kept a set my Aunt Catherine had given me years ago. They are American Limoges, the Hollywood pattern, an almost white color with a gold rim. I can't use them in my new little microwave because the rims are real gold and send off sparks. This set is the first of family treasures I start to use every day, because that's all I have left.

I gave away my regular flatware, too, but I am not entirely without. When Aunt Catherine died, she left me the family silver. I thought that included the flatware, but her cousin Michael, the executor of her estate, told me no, only the larger pieces. My aunt frequently told me stories of people who fought over family items after someone's death, so I decided not to be part of such a story, as if she would be around to hear it or to tell it. Before I went to Thanksgiving at Luke's, I bought a set of silverware in an antique store out on Route 1. It came in a nice velvet-lined wooden box. If someone had said to me, "These are the knives, spoons, and forks your aunt left you," I probably would have believed them. Hers were in a velvet lined box and looked a lot like the ones I bought. For under a hundred dollars, using some of the money she left me, I got what I thought I was getting and kept a bit of dignity.

I have a few silver service sets including creamers, sugars, pitchers, and tea pots along with trays to set them on. It's all silver plate, not sterling. We are Irish Catholic, after all, not old Yankee money. When members of my family, new in this country in the early 1900s, collected this stuff, it was the height of having arrived to have polished silver on the sideboard. Look at me maintaining the illusions that maneuvered into traditions. Admittedly keeping the silver polished is not my cup of tea, but I do like seeing it, at least some of it, in my trailer.

Every box I unpack contains paraphernalia with memories attached. This is taking a long time. There's the Japanese paddle lady, also known as a hagiota fan, given to us by a Japanese exchange student who stayed with us back in the days when we were a family with a home. "I remember you! Good to see you again," I say out loud when she comes out of her box. She is like a doll crafted from the waist up and attached to a black wooden paddle with its own stand. Attired in the style of a geisha, as far as I know, she wears an intricately patterned red kimono and has her black hair piled on her head. We weren't sure what to make of her, but I have always considered her beautiful. She may turn out to be good company here.

I have coffee mugs, a lot of coffee mugs. They became an easy souvenir and a bit of a conversation piece. I didn't deliberately set out to collect them, but I realized I was doing that as the collection grew. Now I have over one hundred of them and each brings a memory.

There's the oldest among them. It's a single mug, a simple design of desert earth colors with a few broad stripes all the way around, below the handle. I bought it for ten lirot in Safat, Israel. I once left it where I was working when Matthew was born. I left the job more suddenly than I planned because I developed preeclampsia and was admitted to the hospital right from a routine doctor's visit. I retrieved the mug on a visit back at my old job with my new baby. When the handle broke off a few years ago, I successfully glued it back on. Now here it is with me.

I have quite a few mugs I received as gifts and a good number of those came from Luke. He knew it was always a safe bet to get me a mug from an Irish import store. One of my favorites says, "IRISH DIPLOMACY *The ability to tell a man to go to hell so that he looks forward to the trip*." He gave me that one right after the divorce.

Others are nicely crafted mugs in shades of blue and green he knew I would like.

Brigid has given me mugs saying O'Leary and Herself. Among those and others I find the old favorite, the Mary Englebreit Design saying simply, SNAP OUT OF IT, repeated in three panels depicting a young lady in a large hat, hands on hips. I bought that one for myself. It's the one I choose when I am trying to chase away my depression.

To the left of the stove the trailer has a pantry closet with the inside of the door all shelves. It's the perfect place for my mug collection. They don't all fit in at once, but I can store them there on a rotating basis with the remaining few on the kitchen window-sill. As I continue to unpack, I'm having coffee in my "The World's Best Mom" mug Matt brought home from an eighth grade trip to Montreal. It won out today over the Smithsonian Museum mug from our stop in Washington, D.C, driving back from a Florida vacation in 1995 - our last vacation as a family.

I like to think I am not attached to things, but I realize every item coming out of these boxes is having its way with me. I decide to move furniture instead.

The bed is in the larger bedroom at the end of the trailer, the room I have decided to use as my office, so I move the mattress and box spring into the hall past the door to the smaller bedroom. I dismantle the bed, wowing myself I can do this. I only have to move the headboard and the frame and then put it back together with the box spring and mattress on top. Before I started the project, I would have thought this would be overwhelming for me, but like so many projects, breaking it apart piece by piece makes it manageable. Who knew?

It seems my kids don't know what to make of this move. Luke hears it as Moral, Maine. I guess he gets that from names like Freedom and Liberty. I want them all to come visit so they will know where I am. My last move was so stressful; I do want them to know this one is much easier.

I have most of my stuff moved in and will be staying here soon, but I have had to put some time into the workshop. My desktop computer is still at Martha's so I am still there quite a bit. I'm doing the workshop this month in Gloucester, Massachusetts, not Newburyport where I usually teach. It's about half an hour to forty minutes extra driving time. On the first of the two Saturdays, it starts to snow during the workshop, but nothing much at first. I think, "Nice. Flurries. Beautiful." I love snow flurries and enjoy driving in a light snow.

On my drive home back to Maine, I stop in Seabrook, New Hampshire, for some household supplies and food. I love that I even *have* a household to supply now. The snow is getting heavier and I know I have three hours of driving ahead of me. I think about calling Cathy to see if I could stay overnight at her house in Amesbury, but decide instead to head for home in Monroe. By the time I'm passing Brunswick the snowstorm has made for bad driving. My sister Jo lives in Brunswick. I wish she were better off, not financially, but in terms of herself. As I go past Brunswick on the highway, I wish my sister could be happier, but life has taken its toll. She had two children who each died as young adults. I imagine what it would be like to go to my sister's house, to warm up and calm down. I would be welcome, but I'm not up to it. Instead I call Martha to see if it is snowing heavily in Monroe. It isn't. Maybe I should get a motel room, but I don't. I beat the storm back to Waldo County.

The following Monday is President's Day, but I forget it is a holiday and go into the Chamber office to do some work there. For the first time ever, I can't get onto the computer. There never was a log-on required before, but now there is. I call the president of the Board of Directors, but she is away for a family matter. After I leave the Chamber office because I can't get anything done, I get a message on my cell phone from the Vice President of the Board asking me to call him. When I do, he asks me if I could be at a meeting at his office in Searsport, north of Belfast, at 10 a.m. the next morning. I say yes, but don't feel good about this situation. Why the mystery?

The next morning I leave Martha's in plenty of time to get to the office in Searsport. I have so much time, I would be too early. I stop in the parking lot of The Chowder House Restaurant for an inspiring view of Penobscot Bay where I joke with myself that all this drama is about telling me I am doing a wonderful job and they want to give me a raise. I know it's a joke. Looking out over the expanse of the bay, I remind myself my mother died when I was ten; I have had breast cancer twice. As long as my kids are okay, it's pretty hard to give me bad news. Whatever this news is, I will be okay, too.

When I get to the meeting, another board member and the Vice President are there. We make small talk about Belfast while we wait for a third member, the same woman who asked me to move my car. I guess she gets to be in on this even if she is late. Once she arrives, I hear the Vice President say to me, "Your services will no longer be needed."

"May I ask why?"

"Goals were not met."

"Well, okay, then."

I remove the keys to the office from my car keys thinking goals were not stated. What difference does it make now? I don't work for these people anymore. I don't ask any further questions, I do not beg to differ, and I do not cry. I say goodbye and leave.

Now I have rented a place of my own and lost the income I was going to use to pay for it. Oh well. I'm moving anyway. I have decided to move and it's my decision, no one else's. I'll have to find another way to make it work.

I head out to Bell the Cat, a Belfast cafe in a bookstore, to get a great cup of coffee and a pastry. Going for a minor splurge won't set me back too much. It was on days like this that I used to go up to the dam in Freedom to sit and think. I could head down to the boathouse in Belfast to look out over the bay again, but first I meet up with one of the board members when she is crossing the same parking lot. She seems as though seeing me might be a little awkward, but I won't have it that way. I like her and I am not going to act embarrassed around town. I give a big smile and say hello.

"Hi, how are you doing?" she asks.

"Well, I got the news this morning, but I'll be okay."

"They just told you today? We met last Thursday."

She looks stunned, even a little embarrassed, but I have no reason to take anything out on her. When they voted me in, they met on a Thursday evening and called me on Friday morning to tell me by phone. When they voted me out, no one called me. They left it until Tuesday morning and called me to a meeting for the pleasure of telling me in person.

The Chamber job hasn't offered me the social contact I expected. In fact, it's caused more social anxiety than connection. When I moved furniture there it became a frustration, yet when I moved it in my new home it was a feeling of success. My life is better than my job. I'll have to go with that idea for now.

# Lost Time

I'm finally about done with the move to Morrill, made especially easier now that I have so much time on my hands. I'm lonely. Even though the Chamber job didn't work out socially, it provided some contact. I had to be there at least twice a week and despite the fact I was usually alone in the office, I did meet up with people occasionally and spoke on the phone a lot. Now I am in the trailer, alone most of the time; this is not good for my mental health.

Fortunately, this weekend all three kids and Matt's girlfriend Gretyl are here for Easter. Brigid has already been here for a few days, coming up early on her own. We get our hair cut, our nails painted, and we go out to eat. We are all dolled up. The boys and Gretyl arrive on Friday and it is great for them to be here, to have them see where I live. The first night we are all together, Brigie and I make salad and bake spinach manicotti bought frozen from Hannaford's Supermarket. Matt must have arrived hungry because he announces he ate his share of the manicotti, even though it had green things in it.

We spend most of Saturday out and about in Belfast. Matt has his laundry with him because he thought I'd have a washer and dryer, so he spends part of his time at the laundromat. We make one trip in two cars back to Martha's and each kid carries at least one plastic bin of fabrics downstairs and out to the vehicles. I take some ribbing about moving these again, but now my move is complete. I once again have these remnants of the memory of my mother, who taught me to sew, back with me where I live.

The kids don't mind sleeping all over the place. Brigid gets the back bedroom/office where she camps out on a sleeping bag along with her dog Wookie. It's best for her to be able to have a door to close so the cats and the dog can be kept apart. I sleep in my own bed, Luke gets the couch while Matt and Gretyl have the living room floor. As I go to sleep, I feel so glad to have them all here. I am proud and grateful they would bother to come.

On Easter Sunday morning, after a huge breakfast including bacon, eggs, and hot cross buns, we make a holiday treat. I saw a recipe for Peeps Pie on the NPR website and have all the ingredients at the ready. It's disgusting, but fun, to watch the yellow marshmallow treats shaped like little chicks melting into a saucepan. The finished product is too, too sweet for me to eat a whole piece of it. We have fun making it together, though, and that is the whole point for me.

For two nights I have all of them with me, but as they pull away from the trailer, back to their own lives, I feel myself shrivel. It's me and the cats again. As good as the weekend has been, the feeling of being complete drains out of me as I sink into the couch alone. I sit and think, but without a water view or pastry, the things that I usually seek to soothe myself. Only Girlfriend senses there is a need to be near me. Maybe she is lonely, too. When I lie down on the sofa, she snuggles on my chest and I'm grateful for the contact.

On Monday morning I wake up tired and lonely, facing the void of my daily life with a kind of automation. First I do this, then I do that, then I am at the computer with a cup of coffee doing a bit of work, slowly. Eventually the day is over.

Losing the Chamber job hurt my cash flow, I'll give them that. I don't miss the people, especially the ones who did not like me. I do miss having some direct contact with people, but mostly, I miss the money. It wasn't a lot, but it was enough to make a difference at the time. Living alone with so little cash is eating me. When I think of things I might like to do, I have no money to do them. Fortunately, because I am not busy with the Chamber, I have more time available for some new work developing through the first-time homebuyer workshop. We will be doing some affordable housing applications and possibly some down payment assistance. It's all in Massachusetts, but I can do a good part of the job from here. I have my office set up with internet access, a land line phone, and my copier/printer/fax/scanner. The phone number I use for business is the same one I've had since I was a RE/MAX agent.

The area code is 978 for northern Massachusetts, but I pick up my messages online. It's not as smooth as being right there, but it works out okay, if not easily.

On a Tuesday morning in early May, I'm having another solitary day working on my computer when I hear a beep. I always thought it would be something bigger. I thought there'd be a thick envelope with lots of papers to sign or maybe a phone call would come first to make sure they had my correct address. But it's a beep.

There is no one around and it's so quiet here, alone in this two-bedroom mobile home. I tell people I live in a trailer in a field in Maine. The birds usually make the most noise. From my back bedroom office, I can hear someone mowing a lawn, but remember lawn mowers don't have horns. I hear a knock at the door, my door. Who knows I'm here? These days even my public self is pretty much incognito. At the door is the mail lady – I know that's incongruous – she's the female mail lady.

"You have a package. Postage due. $2.07."

I look at the small package wrapped in white paper partially ripped. The return address is NNER, but in my mind I transpose it to NNRE. I think it has something to do with real estate, so I say I'll take it. I'm surprised someone sent real estate pamphlets to this address, but it's believable.

I tell the woman, "Well this proves I'll pay $2.07 out of curiosity." As I hand her a pile of change I counted out to make the full amount, she laughs. She seems glad to get rid of the package.

Taking the little bundle into the kitchen, I open it to find five identical booklets. Still thinking it has something to do with my first-time homebuyer's workshop, I'm surprised to see poetry inside. I look at the return address again and it says, NNER, Northern New England Review. I have submitted some writing to them; maybe they are sending me contributor copies. I never got a thick envelope or a phone call or even an email. Who am I kidding? Contributor copies. I do have in my hands five copies of their latest issue. A quick look to the index doesn't show me my name; maybe they sent copies to everyone who submitted. No. These small literary journals never do that. Maybe they are sample copies so I'll subscribe. No, they had to pay $2.07 to send these to me. I had to pay $2.07 because they were forwarded from Monroe to Morrill. I look inside again. They have a poem called "Cat's Gone". I have a poem called "Cat's Gone" and there's my name in the book next to the title of the poem. I quickly remind myself when I look for my name in an index, I should look more carefully. It could be there. I turn to page 43 and see Cat's Gone by Ellie O'Leary. I'm published! I'm a published poet! Not with a bang, but a beep. There's a contributor's note about me in the back of the book. Those seem like words I wrote or would have written, but the phrases now appear with lots of quotation marks. I would not have sent in a note in that format, but what do I care now?

Home alone, living alone. How to celebrate? First I tell Buddha and Girlfriend, but since they're cats I give them treats. Now we all know it's a good day. I move on to emailing. Starting with my personal support group, I tell Cathy, Carol, and Margaret attaching the poem to the email. I realize I forgot Mooncat and Mimi from the writing retreat at Pyramid so I forward the email to them, too. I call each kid, so three phone calls right there. I leave three messages.

No one emails me back instantly. Okay. I decide to go into Belfast figuring I can make calls on my cell phone. First I pick up a few groceries at Hannaford's. No one recognizes me as a published poet, but I move on to the cafe, Bell the Cat. There I order myself a panini sandwich to go. It's a great sandwich and despite the fact I have to be so careful about money, especially since I got voted out by the Chamber, I did get published. I'll celebrate if I want. I drive down to a space by the boathouse and eat alone. It occurs to me if anyone loved me, a man for instance, we could go to dinner at the restaurant called Darby's. It's local food with an international influence; I think that's called fusion now. I went there with my friend Carol when she came to visit me in Monroe and once with Martha. I like the food and the atmosphere. That's where I really want to go, but not alone. I might afford it alone, but I cannot afford to treat anyone. If I had a circle of friends around here, we could do that. If anyone in Belfast loved me or cared, we could go to Darby's. Instead I'm eating a sandwich alone in my car, but I have my celebration. I savor it.

Slowly things in general seem to be getting better. With careful planning I have managed to get out of my own way by signing up for classes in Pilates, Workshop Facilitation, and Sewing with a Serger. I looked for inexpensive classes and found them in the local adult education scene. There is nothing about any of these topics making a big difference to me, but it is a way to get out. It gives me a local schedule.

Brigid has an end of year figure skating show at the rink where she coaches in Greenfield, Massachusetts. I've been pleased to have that to look forward to and to share with her. Her students will be skating and she will do a solo program. A few days before the show itself she calls me because, including one for her solo, she is getting two new skating dresses and new tires on the same day. She is in desperate need of the new tires, but the shop with the dresses may be closing earlier than the tire shop.

"Which one should I go to first?" she asks.

It makes me feel useful to point out the obvious.

"Go to the tire shop. Go early enough so you still have time to get the dresses." She has to know that, but I can't help feeling good she asked me.

Like at Christmas, I go out to her place a day before everyone else in the family. As is the tradition, I have flowers with me to present to her right after she gets off the ice following her solo, but, as is the tradition, she is not supposed to see them until after the show. Before I knock on her door to say I'm here, I hide my flowers at the top of the basement stairs. Her landlords live in the other apartment in the house and their daughters skate, too, so I know they will understand why the flowers are there. They will not mention any flowers to her if they do notice them.

I came here in a low mood, but the show is a lot of fun for all of us. Some of her friends from Amesbury, and most of her family including her dad and his wife have come. Her student group skates out wearing one costume, not the same costume, but actually one costume. They are a multi-colored caterpillar. At the end of the show she does her solo in a silver sleek new dress, lands all her jumps and shines.

She gets off the ice beaming. "That was fun!"

No anxiety here, not today, not for either one of us. Back at her apartment we order Chinese - one of the things we do when we resemble a big happy family.

# Down Time

When I moved into Martha's house, I was grateful. I remain grateful and realize even more now, I was fortunate to live with her rather than alone. I realize this because living alone again is nearly killing me. I've been lonely before; being this lonely is what I knew as a child. Even going to school every day was no cure because the feeling was part of my core. Just as when my kids pulled away from here to go home after Easter, the shades can come down quickly in my head and loneliness rises up, settles in.

At Martha's we could always get into a conversation – what she did at work, something in the news, anything about our kids. We're both talkers and that was good; that was helpful. Here I do more thinking than talking, and it's not working out well.

Why am I even from this area where I have no relatives and most everyone else seems to have a cousin down the road in any direction? That's the way it was in Freedom. When I moved there, three of the ten kids in my fifth grade class might have seemed to have nothing in common. Two of them were brother and sister, and they were first cousins with another one. I might have thought they wouldn't really know each other except in a town of about four hundred people, of course they did. Their mothers were sisters. Really. First cousins. Tommy was first cousins with Louise and Everett. All the kids in the village seemed to be cousins to each other or someone nearby, all of them except me and my brother Danny. We only had our parents and we didn't have our mother there for long, just a few months.

Even though I believe kids should have a mother, I've learned over the years that maybe having a mother isn't everything. There are kids with mothers who aren't happy, but I still would have welcomed the opportunity to have mine, to find out for myself, in the flesh, right there at home. Since most kids did have mothers, I interpreted that to mean I couldn't have what most people had.

That was an important lesson for me and it's how I got by. As long as I accepted that I couldn't have what other people did, my life was manageable. I discounted what I did have. I was bright, in good health, and even had a sense of humor although I didn't know the word *sardonic* back in my Freedom Village days. What I had, I didn't appreciate because it's what I had and I came by those things with no effort.

As a teenager I focused on what I didn't have – the right clothes, the right things to say. When I started to outgrow my clothes, I found some of my mother's skirts in an old trunk and started to wear those rolled up at the waist because they were still too long. One was a pretty lavender and another was a dark blue with a border print. Why did my father let me do that? I should have had my own clothes, but I should have had my own name, too. I was the living Helen O'Leary wearing the dead Helen O'Leary's clothes. I felt invisible, not real, though I was the one still on earth.

Being the awkward one without a mother continued. In college when one of the girls in my dorm got engaged, I offered congratulations and was promptly told in front of a group of us in the rec room, "That's not what you say." Apparently, you are supposed to say, "Best wishes." or something like that because congratulations sounds like she was trying to snare a man and was successful. I slipped away back to my room, mortified, leaving all the well-dressed coeds with their matching Pendleton sweaters and skirts behind me.

I don't think lonely kids are loud. Maybe angry kids are. This lonely kid was not loud; this lonely kid sat up to Freedom Pond reading, or on the tree stump in front of my house thinking, or in my room crying. This lonely kid did not speak up. This lonely kid put up.

## Senior College

I heard about Senior College, a University of Maine local enrichment program for older residents, when I first came back to Maine, but had trouble connecting. You only have to be fifty years old and pay a membership fee of twenty-five dollars a year.

I checked out the Belfast program online and called the phone number but got no answer to the message I left. By the time I finally stopped in at the Hutchinson Center where the classes meet, the semester had started the week before. The young lady I spoke to told me nobody from Senior College was there that day, only on Thursdays. She also said it was too late to join. I was saddened to say the least and I wonder how things might have been if I had joined earlier.

By the start of the next term I did sign up and doing so goes in the gratitude column of life. Once I finally made the connection, I found where I belong. I only wish I had become involved sooner, but I'm going with the gratitude that I belong to Senior College now.

So far I have taken a nature course and curling. Yes, curling. Brooms and round things on ice. Belfast has the only curling club in Maine. This surprises me, but I'm grateful it's here. Although I've always liked dancing and been pretty good at it, I'm not athletic. I first tried field hockey in gym class in college. One day as I was walking by the same field, I saw an actual game. I was stunned there were girls who played voluntarily. I hated running around a field with other girls, girls carrying big sticks, chasing me. They were yelling at me. Even the coach was yelling, "Sticks! Sticks!" When I did a semester of fencing, I was struck with the absurdity of Honey O'Leary from Freedom, Maine, dressed in padded white, hearing *en garde,* then lunging with an épée. The kids in the village thought it was great to own a decent baseball bat.

Curling could be a better fit. The scoring is intricate, and I like that it is complicated. The techniques are more like chess on ice; I hear it is frowned upon to compare it to shuffleboard. The first weekly session is in a classroom at the Hutchinson Center; we learn terms and scoring. The round thing is called the stone, the circle where it is headed is called the house, the broom is called that even though it doesn't actually look so much like a regular broom. I'm eager to get started on the ice, but the second week of the term I get to the curling club a little late for our first week on the ice. The door is locked. I bang and bang, but no one answers. I can see cars in the parking lot so I know people are in there. I hit the door as hard as I can. I yell, but I still get no answer. I have always had A Little Match Girl Complex; feeling on the outside looking in is a definite trigger for my depression. Although I can't see into the club, I'm locked out. I wasn't thinking it would be like catching a bus; if you are late the bus would be gone. After I bang and scream one last time, I leave. Crying.

The next week I make sure to get back there in plenty of time and easily get in. I can see by the construction of the building the people inside who are actually curling are nowhere near the entrance and couldn't possibly have heard me at the door the previous week. As I start to relate my experience how and why I missed the last session, I feel myself welling up in the telling of it. Now I feel embarrassed and weak, but I'm here. I am going to try curling since I have finally made it this far.

It's a great and pleasant surprise to me that curling is so much fun and, even more, I'm fairly good at it for a rank beginner. In the last of the few sessions we have I am, along with a few others, invited back to join the Belfast Curling Club. I get so excited I buy the T shirt, the pint glass, and even the potholder with the logo. I want to belong to something and these items seem like a nice little, not too expensive, reward to myself.

Curling, though, is not for me in the long run. I'm disappointed I didn't ever try it until this year. My knees are so arthritic, I have to use an extension on the broom. I want to do the smooth low glide I've seen on TV, but can't. I may have been invited back because I understand the scoring, the strategy involved to place my stone in the house closest to the center of the circle while carefully knocking the opposite team's stones away. Again, I'm brains over brawn. Not bad, I guess. It is who I am.

Another reason I can't join is plain old money. Besides paying for my membership I would need my own curling broom and smooth soled shoes, as well as entrance fees and travel expenses to participate in the bonspiels, the tournaments. Even minimal travel is too much. Being the only Maine curling club means the Belfast Curling Club ends up travelling or hosting with clubs in New Brunswick. Sounds nice, but I have to decline. I may be able to keep up with the sport, but now especially without the money from the Chamber job, I am not able to consider those expenses.

Since moving to Morrill and becoming painfully lonely again, I have signed up for anything vaguely interesting to me, if I can afford it. The most expensive of these is a course on Facilitation Skills at the Waldo County Extension Center and it's also the closest to being academic. We discuss how to hold meetings, present reports, and offer programs to a membership or other group. It meets every other week and certainly is not exciting, but I want to get out and have no place to go. The classes give me a schedule plus a chance to talk to someone other than Buddha and Girlfriend. Besides this class I've done Pilates at my old high school and Sewing with a Serger at the high school in Belfast. Of all the things I try, the place that helps me the most and really gets me back into conversation with other people is Senior College. The curling sessions were outside the norm; most sessions meet in a classroom. - right where I belong; right where I am most comfortable. I have already signed up to two courses at Senior College this summer, both of them writing classes.

# Still Trying

I'm still trying to sign up for things that are free or nearly so. Sometimes the only person I speak to is the cashier at the grocery checkout line at Hannaford's. They are all very nice, but I wouldn't call it the start of a friendship.

After coming home from teaching the first-time homebuyer workshop over the weekend, I'm here alone and it is not going well. I amuse myself by feeding a stray ginger cat using the gold-trimmed Limoges dinnerware given to me by Aunt Catherine. The landlady here told me she thinks the previous tenants abandoned their tabby when they moved out. That would explain why this cat keeps trying to get in. My cats, though, are having none of that. I feed the stray by putting some food outside.

I'm stuck here for ten days home alone; my next project to go anywhere won't be until I go back to Massachusetts for a routine doctor's appointment. I sit on the old sofa shapeshifting into it. I've tried to be okay, but my plans are not working. I have barely any food in the house and scarcely any money. I do have a Staples rewards check, a credit for previous purchases. I could use that to buy some food like a plastic container of pretzels, the kind of food the store sells for an office break room. The closest Staples is too far away to make that a reasonable option. It would be a waste of gas. Everything about me seems to be a waste.

Each of my kids are in my thoughts as I try to picture them without me. How will they deal with my decision to not try anymore. Will they be able to understand that I did try, but got tired, more than tired, fatigued? Where are they in their lives that still having an accessible mother would continue to make a difference? Should I make plans for the cats, Buddha and Girlfriend?

I don't know what to do next, so I don't make any definite plans.

# To Party or Not

There have been tragedies in the world since I came back to Maine, including the Indian Ocean tsunami that killed thousands, many of whom disappeared into the waters that rose up and took them away days after my kids and I celebrated a really decent Christmas in Monroe. One evening the following August, when I was staying overnight at Matt's house I told him, "It looks like New Orleans is going to get a big storm." I wasn't going for an understatement or hyperbole. I was thinking more in terms of solidarity and gratitude. It sounded awful even before the storm hit, before mention of the levees breaching. We get hurricanes in New England, but not so much that we are known for them. As much as I'm grateful these disasters have not touched me personally, they have added to my feeling that things can be both pointless and precious. Even though I have been physically safe, I still feel the weight of a thousand winds keeping me down. I'm still dreary on a sunny day.

While this looms large within me, I tell myself that others don't notice. I present a decent exterior or think I do until I have my routine doctor's appointment in early June. My plan is to have the visit in Boston, stay at my friend Cathy's, and then maybe go to Matt's twenty-ninth birthday party the next day in Portsmouth. That's my plan, but perhaps it was the way I said I might not go to my son's party that triggered the response from my doctor. Maybe it was the answer I gave when she asked if I feel I would hurt myself or others. I told her that no, I would never hurt anyone else. I thought my answer was succinct and honest. She asked me for the phone number of the friend where I'd be staying. I sort of dozed off when she left the room briefly returning with a psychiatrist who asked more questions in the same vein. We discussed what to do next. Hospitalization seemed to be an option, to them anyway, but I said it would scare my kids. My doctor said she had spoken to my friend Cathy who would be waiting for me when I got back to Amesbury. All this because I said I thought my son would only want young, happy people at his afternoon ice cream smorgasbord party. As I left the appointment my doctor told me, "Go to your son's party. He invited you."

Late afternoon when I get to Cathy's she says she is going out to some commitment long planned, but our friend Carol would be coming over to visit with me. I have a babysitter. They both sort of pretend it's because Carol and I haven't seen each other for a while. Really. I wouldn't commit suicide in someone else's house, as bad as I feel about myself now, but I appreciate them caring. I feel gratitude, real gratitude, and don't have to pretend.

The next day I go to Matt's birthday party and wonder why I thought I wouldn't go. The offering of a few flavors of ice cream with a variety of toppings is a hit with his friends and I'm reminded that's something we did with kids' birthdays back at the big house where we lived in Amesbury. He goes out later with his friends, and I head up the highway back to my place.

All is well until I get back home and sink into the sofa again.

# Different at Home

It's Father's Day here in the trailer. Probably Father's Day everywhere in the U.S., but I'm feeling it here. I think of going to visit my parents' graves, but I didn't go on Mother's Day. If I were to play favorites, it wouldn't be in that direction.

Daddy didn't really know me even though there was just the two of us in the house for my last two years of high school. My brother graduated before me and a week later was off to the Great Lakes Training Center of the US Navy. I was left at home, my body already morphing into the sprint position getting ready to make my own exit. One of Daddy's expressions was, "You're not out with the gang now." We lived in Freedom Village; there was no gang. There was maybe almost enough kids to make a small gang, but we didn't. What would be the point of that? Harassing each other's parents? Breaking into homes? Too easy, nobody locked their doors. So, no gang.

At home I was stuck being raised by a man who was born in Ireland in 1903 in Cork City. When I talked about school, he'd say things like, "The Christian Brothers didn't do it that way." He occasionally talked about Ireland, but not as much as I'd wished. If he were around now, I'd grill him with questions. He left as a young man, a stowaway on a boat headed to Canada. Why? Did he have to leave in a hurry? Was he part of some Irish Republican activity, something otherwise criminal, or was he, too, sprinting away from a life he didn't want?

Sometimes he could go for days without speaking to me, but one day when I was ironing something, after I set up the ironing board next to the table where he was seated, he did talk. He told me my sister Josephine had always been his favorite. Who says that to their child? Fortunately, I didn't find it insulting. It wasn't a shock, just a revelation, so I found it liberating. No sense trying to please him. He's the only parent I have left, and he's just told me someone else is his favorite. I'll graduate, too, and like my brother, I'll leave.

In the village we lived next door to my high school principal, Mr. Cosgrove, and his family. I always figured if someone had to live next to the principal, it might as well be me. It didn't crimp my style, as if I had any. He called me Helen at school and Honey as a neighbor. One day early in my senior year, he came to our door to talk to my father about something. I forget what the topic was, but the conversation got around to me and what I should be planning to do next. My father asked, "I heard they are starting a college in Unity. Do you think they'd take her?" as if I were some sort of marginal student who could possibly have a shot at a place that was trying to get up and running. I've always loved Charlie Cosgrove's response, "We think she can do better."

One of my high school teachers and his wife, a substitute teacher, both went to Bates College, where they met. Their father (and father-in-law) was Brooks Quimby, the debating coach and speech professor at Bates. When he came to address an assembly at Mount View High School, I was chosen to introduce him. A part of me thinks that was why he was there. Mrs. Quimby, the substitute, happened (?) to be there that day. She introduced me to him saying, "Dad, this is the girl we've been telling you about. We think she'd make a lovely Bates student." A few weeks later a letter came to the high school addressed to me from Professor Quimby saying he had looked at my application and would be recommending I should be accepted. My next-door neighbors, the Cosgroves, happened to be from Lewiston, Maine, where Bates is located. Mrs. Cosgrove told me she would be going to visit her mother one day and perhaps I would like to make an appointment to visit Bates. Again looking back, that's all really nice and supportive. I've wondered since which came first, her plans to visit her mother or plans to help me to visit Bates. After the visit, when I told my father there are maids in the dorms who come in once a week, he told me not to get too full of myself. He never, not once, told me he was proud of me or congratulated me.

Even the day the actual Bates acceptance came, I was complimented, but not overly excited. To get the mail in Freedom, I'd go up the hill to the post office. If there was mail too big for our box, like the acceptance package had been, there would be a notice in the box to present at the service counter. The day my financial aid package came, I finally let go. I opened it right there in the post office immediately after the postmistress, Avis Evans, handed it to me. Even now when I drive by, I joke with myself that I'm surprised the little, gray, one-story clapboard building is still standing after my enthusiastic response. Getting accepted was nice; getting substantial financial aid was my ticket into Bates and my ticket out of the village. I was crouching further into the sprint position and towards my exit.

That was such an exciting time, so full of promise, making the time I'm having now all the more disappointing, shameful, and embarrassing. Sometimes I dip back into these memories of promising times, but they don't make me feel better. They eat away at me, making me feel worse, leading me to the painful memories, the reasons I knew I would leave.

When I was eleven I read something in *Good Housekeeping* magazine about girls bleeding. When it first happened to me, I told my father I had blood in my pants. He told me to go up to the store and talk to Mollie. Archie and Mollie Knight owned the IGA store in town right near our house, on the corner at the bottom of Academy Hill. She was always nice to me and let me hang out with her sometimes in the store. I even got the occasional free Three Musketeers candy bar. When I showed up that day, she got me Kotex pads and the elastic belt to hold them. I'm thinking she must have offered to him beforehand that she would help out at a time like this since he came up with what to do, where to go, so quickly.

There was something different at home, too. After this change in me, he stopped putting his hand in my pants while looking at my face, looking to see if I might like it. I did not. As a younger kid after my mother died, I had slipped into bed with him a few times if I couldn't sleep or had a scary dream, but I didn't know people did that to each other in bed. I didn't like that either. As I got older, he did leave me alone, but I never really felt safe at home. I wonder sometimes what he meant when he said Jo was his favorite, but I'll never know. She doesn't talk much about such things. She told me once about ten years ago that a neighbor, a friend of my parents, had molested her but when she told them, they didn't believe her. That would have happened before I was born. I've always thought Jo teetered indelicately between strong and fragile, but her drinking makes it hard to ask questions. She only talks once she's had some alcohol, but the tales she tells then don't always make sense. Some things I remember, too, and it's best to say we remember them differently. She once asked me how I could have Mommy's picture hanging in my house. Didn't I know what she was like? No, I didn't apparently. Clearly Jo and I remember her differently. I'm sure we each remember each parent differently.

I have wondered what it would have been like if my mother had been the parent who lived longer. Would I have learned at least a few more social graces? I don't know. When my time to leave Freedom came at last, I went off into the world knowing I was nobody's favorite at home, but grateful for the support I had received at my school.

# Writing

This summer I have been able to take two courses at Senior College, each one taught by one of a couple from Texas. Texas? I didn't expect to meet anyone from Texas, but two of the nicest people I have ever met are Gary and Priscilla Tate. They are retired English professors who spend the summer in Belfast and I readily sign up for their literary offerings. In his course on working class poetry Gary Tate is using the anthology *Working Classics: Poems on Industrial Life*. It even includes a poem in the book about a Sister Monica who takes her young students on a field trip to a factory, reminding me of our Sister Monica who runs Pyramid Life Center. Gary introduces the term *genteel poverty*, but I hear it as *gentile poverty* and think I'm in on two counts. I didn't know either term – gentile or genteel – when I was growing up, but I can see that genteel poverty is a good description of what we were. One day in Freedom Grammar School, one of my classmates had some cards he got in some sort of set. They were like the sayings you might get in a fortune cookie, but on a card a bit bigger. He put one on each kid's desk and mine said – *If you're so smart, why ain't you rich?* I've thought of that often over the years, especially these last few.

Priscilla Tate is teaching memoir and I'm thrilled to be in the class. When each of us gets a chance to read what we've been working on, I get exuberant, wave my hand in the air, and get to go first. I read my new piece about the night I couldn't find my fabrics at my son's house. I'm expecting nods, maybe polite thank-yous, or ancillary questions and comments such as "My mother used to sew my clothes." or "Do you make quilts?" Instead, they are rapt, actually listening. Priscilla tells me it is very good. I feel alive.

Despite feeling alive in class, back home I deflate again. There's me, the cats, and maybe a cup of coffee or tea. When I try to get up off the couch, there's something much heavier than a cat holding me down. The invisible weight of my depression keeps me sunk into the couch cushions taking my breath and voice away. This isn't something an inhaler can cure. This is deeper inside me than my lungs and more systemic than air itself. I still don't know what to do next, but I'm going to have to figure something out.

I finally admit to myself that living alone in this trailer is not the right thing for me. I don't think I can afford anything back home in the Amesbury area and hearing myself think like that, I realize I don't know where home is. Is it where I am or where my people are, the living ones who love me? I keep thinking I should make plans, but I feel exhausted. I've been making plans, doing check-lists, figuring things out for the last two years. Even longer than that, but for the last two years especially. Apparently, I'm not done yet, but it's time once more to go to the women's writing retreat. Just like I used to sit up to the dam on Freedom Pond, I can sit next to the lake at Pyramid to see if I can figure things out. Make some plans.

I can't afford to go to the retreat, but I can't afford not to go either so I register, even though there's still a part of me saying I don't deserve to go. When I mention to my friend Cathy that I'm going to look for a cheap place to live in the Amesbury area, sure enough she knows of something that someone in her office has listed for rent. She says it's on the top floor of a company on Route 1 in Salisbury, one town over from Amesbury. The access is behind the building. Before heading out all the way to the retreat, I drive behind the address in Salisbury and try to picture myself coming home after dark, going behind a building, alone, to get to an apartment. I can't figure out which door it might be. Each of the businesses seems to have a door, maybe for a fire exit or maybe it's where they put their trash out. It unnerves me a bit to think of this setting, but I do. I'm not in a position to be fussy.

The retreat itself is another success. Not a booming literary experience but another renewal of friendships and some writing. I even get a new coffee mug that is part of the registration that year. Once back from the retreat I make an appointment to see the studio apartment in Salisbury, but discover I was behind the wrong address when I went by myself to check it out. The correct entry is in a well-lit parking lot behind a nearby building. The apartment, compared to what I was expecting, is stunning. It's a hot day and the air conditioning is on. I find myself thinking this could do nicely. Very nicely. I say yes to the apartment and go back to Maine to make plans to move again.

This new apartment isn't quite ready for a tenant as they have to do a few other things to make it a separate space including blocking off a doorway that would lead to the company's offices. I'm a combination of excited and exhausted, so it's good to have some time to get myself organized.

## On the Road Again

All my stuff gets packed up again. Some of it never got un-packed since I haven't fully set up my office and lots of kitchen things have been in boxes since the lake house in Amesbury. I'm not able to rent a truck because I have left calling around until too late. I'm afraid to give my debit card number because there was not enough money in the account as I was making the calls and I'm not sure when they actually charge the card. I have no viable credit card. For most places I call, I leave a message, don't actually talk to anyone anyway. On the Saturday of the move Matt and Gretyl arrive in Morrill with his motorcycle trailer in tow. Martha comes over to say goodbye and to help out. As they drive away the trailer sags from the weight of all my things causing me to think maybe I should have thrown much of it away. We wonder how far they'll get, but I give them my key since they should get to the new place first, as long as the trailer holds up. I say goodbye to Martha and thank her repeatedly for all she's done, most recently stopping in here to feed the cats when I was at the retreat and even coming over here today. Without her I'd be nowhere. I'm not sure where I am now, but I'm headed somewhere again, once more starting over.

Matt, with the trailer intact, makes it to Salisbury just fine. I have told him to go behind the building and up the outside stair-case on the left. At first he has trouble getting the key to work, so he calls me telling me he leaned over to look in a window and it looks like an office. He thinks he may be in the wrong place. That's believable since I went to the wrong place first, but his description tells me he's there. I tell him he's got it right. The office space is on the second floor, but the apartment is on the third. Once he gets the door open, he'll be facing another set of stairs inside.

Matt tries the key in the door again and is still on the phone with me when he walks in and goes up the inside staircase. "Oh, Mom, congratulations!"

Huh, congratulations. I haven't heard that a lot lately, but here I go again. Once I get there I spend the first night in an empty apartment with two confused cats.

The next day we all meet up to unload the trailer. Luke and Brigid are equally impressed and things are looking good. From the third floor there is a sliding door to a small deck, with no steps down, on the back of the building. From there I see a view of the saltmarsh next to the Merrimac River and soon learn I have some beautiful sunsets to view. I know almost immediately that this is the right place for me while I get myself reorganized, straightened out. I don't know how long I'll stay here. It's a bit awkward living above a business, but at least I am closer to my kids. Matt's in Portsmouth, Luke's in Cambridge, and Brigid has rented a small apartment in nearby Newburyport. We are close enough to see each other often, without making an overnight trip of it.

I wonder how many times I'm going to move back and forth to Maine. The first time in November of 1958, when we moved from Massachusetts to Maine, set me on that track. I associated the move with great loss, blaming the move for the loss, as if we could move back to Somerville and Mommy would be there. I knew she wouldn't be, it was just an "as if." Loss became a life theme though and I think Janis Joplin summed it up when she sang *Freedom's just another word for nothing left to lose.* Kris Kristofferson wrote it. She sang it. I felt it.

In the spring of 2004 when I lost my grip, if I even had one, it seemed natural to go back to the land of loss. Now this move, this return to the living, is by my own decision and I hope I'm right. I'll have to make the best choices I can with the options I have. Continuing to choose what will move me forward to mental and physical health is what I have going for myself now. So far, this return to friends and family feels right and gives me hope.

# Epilogue

## Living in Gravy

In early January 2016, as I walked onto an Aer Lingus flight to Dublin, I felt myself welling up. In 2004 I had gone home to Maine thinking I had come to so much of nothing, thinking I might have gone home to die, and then thinking that I might actually facilitate that by causing my own death. Instead there I was boarding a flight that would take me to Ireland to do a residency in Howth as a part of my MFA program. I was finally getting that advanced degree that I never got before. I was working toward my Master of Fine Arts with a concentration in poetry and was headed to Ireland for a few weeks. I appreciated the distance I had come from being locked into myself by depression to being able to make plans, good plans, and follow through. I called that trip my victory lap and was so pleased with how far I had managed to travel emotionally, from sinking into a sofa in defeat, to boarding a plane on my first international experience since cancer, divorce, and bankruptcy were the highlights of my to-do list.

As I write this in 2022 I consider the times I've been through since Matt congratulated me on finding a decent apartment. There have been some losses, including all of the pets mentioned in this story except Matt's cat Cammie who lives on at twenty years old. We've lost my mentor Mooncat, my sister-in-law Judie, my Senior College friend Gary Tate, and Sister Monica who ran the Pyramid Life Center. My sister Josephine passed away on her birthday in December 2016. Prior to that she had lost both of her children and her husband. I settled her estate and found out how much heart-breaking work can be involved in that endeavor, particularly closing out her house to get it ready to sell. My sister Barbara is now the most recent to leave us after declining health and being in home hospice at her daughter's house.

There have also been gains. I officiated at my daughter's wedding on the beach at Plum Island in Newburyport, Massachusetts, and now have not only a son-in-law but two grandchildren, Gavin and Ananda.

Besides going to Ireland in 2016, I also went there in 2017 to attend the Cork International Poetry Festival, and again in 2019 on my own for a personal writing retreat, visiting both Cork and Dublin. My friend Alwina started spending weeks in Paris each Fall. She said to me, "I'm going to Paris. Why don't you pop over?" I did -- in 2017 and in 2018.

As for that apartment that I thought would do nicely while I got myself straightened out, I stayed there six years until the company downstairs decided to expand up into the space I was renting. Moving there was my own decision, not one imposed on me by circumstances. I hoped it would be a good decision and it was, even though it looked and felt like a temporary space and that's how I thought of it as each year clicked by. I never referred to it as home despite how much I loved it there. It always felt temporary so I didn't change my legal address, including my car registration, from Martha's house in Monroe and I returned there often. I even completed jury duty in Belfast. When I did have to move in 2013, I rented another great apartment, this time in Topsham, Maine, which seemed to be about halfway from everywhere I was going. Halfway from Amesbury to Belfast, halfway to Greenville where my sister Jo was. She had previously lived near Topsham and still had medical appointments in the area. She would stay with me, and we went to her appointments together as her health was declining. I was living in Topsham and stayed after Josephine died, but in late 2017 I moved back to Amesbury to be near my family and friends, but especially to be near my grandchildren. I now live a few blocks from them in a small house I've been able to buy.

Senior College worked out so well, I started teaching writing classes there including poetry, memoir, and a multi-genre class. When someone wanted a class on writing legacy letters, the curriculum committee asked me to teach it and I did, after I looked up legacy letters. A woman in one of my writing classes told me she was taking a medical leave of absence from her monthly radio show Writers Forum on WERU, a community radio station, and asked if I'd like to fill in for her. When she decided not to do the show anymore, I took it over and did it for three years. The station was north of Belfast and not convenient to get to, especially when I was renting in Salisbury, Massachusetts, but I loved doing it. I only stopped because it was too much once I started the MFA program. I've continued to attend the Women's Writing Retreat and started to teach poetry there, too. I also started a new program at the same retreat center, one for both men and women. I knew better than to do it alone so I recruited my friend Nelle Stanton, and we co-founded the Fall Writerfest. In 2020 I became the Poet Laureate of Amesbury, Massachusetts, and published my first book of poetry *Breathe Here,* just before the pandemic started.

My work as a first-time home buyer counselor increased as we took on additional programs such as down payment assistance and applications for affordable housing. I became the Executive Director of Coastal Homebuyer Education, which has been much better than being the Associate Executive Director of the Chamber in Belfast. I was earning enough to be solvent, could easily pay the rent in the studio apartment, and by the time I moved to the larger apartment in Topsham, I was doing well enough to have a small savings.

These years since 2006 have reminded me of my plan after that first cancer surgery, when I decided to live the years my mother did not have, for both of us. If I made it to age fifty-six and beyond, it would be all gravy after that. Although the plan did not work out that way at first, bit by bit, day by day, I got stronger and became fully engaged with living a better life.

I can't say I found a cure for anything that ailed me, but I can say I managed to get out of my own way by repeatedly asking myself what to do next. I worked to discover what would move me forward in the next direction I wanted to go. When I'm asked how things got better for me, I don't have a tight answer. Getting better, being happier, and at least somewhat more successful in measurable, observable ways, took time and perseverance. Noticing what triggered my depression and what might make my day easier were essential considerations for my well-being, but better results were achieved through trial and error over a period of years. Earning sufficient income, not based on commission, and being near family and friends were major factors. Most importantly, I constantly asked myself what I should do next so that I was making plans in the direction I wanted to go.

I decided to do the MFA program even though that meant borrowing some money, which I don't regret. Getting the MFA opened up my world and contributed to the confidence that now keeps me from sinking into the furniture as a sorry loss. I move forward recognizing that I still have some of the same situations. I still have my asthmatic coughing and sneezing fits and I still sometimes detach from real life into an episode of depression. I have the capacity, after lots of experience, to recognize the depression and work my way out. I'm checked for breast cancer at least once a year and have had only a few minor scares including the time I checked my voicemail while in Paris and heard there was something suspicious on my mammogram. I had it done again after I got home and was cleared. My family has been spared the worst of the pandemic. For now I'm still living in gravy with gratitude.

# Acknowledgements

Heartfelt thanks to my editor, Ted Deppe, to my beta readers Pam Clements, Sue Cummings, Maxene Kupperman-Guiñals, Kay Patterson, and Nelle Stanton, to workshop leaders Meredith Hall and Monica Wood of the Maine Writers and Publishers Alliance and to Marion Roach Smith and other writers of Pyramid Lake in the Women's Writing Retreat and the Fall Writerfest including Clif Travers. Special acknowledgement to the late Carol Glover who urged me on and on.


An earlier form of Chapter 7 was previously published in *Buddy Lit Zine* as "Situations."

Back Cover Photo: Easter Weekend 2006
Photo credit to Gretyl Macalaster

www.ingramcontent.com/pod-product-compliance
Lightning Source LLC
Chambersburg PA
CBHW052104090426
42741CB00009B/1669